TEACHING
REBELLION

TEACHING
REBELLION

Stories from the Grassroots
Mobilization in Oaxaca

Edited by Diana Denham & C.A.S.A. Collective

PMPRESS

TEACHING REBELLION

Stories from the Grassroots Mobilization in Oaxaca

By Diana Denham and the C.A.S.A. Collective

Published by:
PM Press
PO Box 23912
Oakland, CA 94623
www.pmpress.org

Cover photograph by Eleuterio García
Layout and design by Diana Denham & Courtney Utt

ISBN: 978-1-60486-032-0
Library Of Congress Control Number: 2008929100

10 9 8 7 6 5 4 3 2 1

Printed in the USA on recycled paper.

TABLE OF CONTENTS

ACKNOWLEDGEMENTS

We are grateful to all of the people who have dared to imagine, defy, create and march under the banner of a more just Oaxaca. We are especially indebted to those who have shared with us their dreams and struggles so that we can share them with others through this book.

For advice, questions, contacts and encouragement we thank Silvia Hernández Salinas, Gustavo Vilchis, Sergio Beltrán, Anabel López Sánchez, Sara Méndez, Diego Cruz Martínez, Jonathan Treat and Ilaria Gabbi. We thank Yakira Teitel and Peter Gelderloos for their extremely valuable revisions. Many thanks to the C.A.S.A. board and Anna-Reetta Korhonen, Kate Iris Hilburger, and Claire Urbanski for their contributions to a nascent collective in uncertain circumstances.

We are especially grateful to Rights Action, Squat Elimäenkatu 15, Terrace F. Club, Glen Brown and Jeanie and Kate Benward, whose generous support made possible the book's first printing. Thanks to Matt Burke and Gwen Meyer for help with photos, layout and printing ideas, and thanks to the Oaxaca Solidarity Network and Rebeca Jasso Aguilar for helping with transcriptions.

We also want to express our appreciation of Doña Angelina for keeping us well-fed with tamales and for up-to-the-minute reports on neighborhood news and the radio's latest broadcasting. Compiling this book has been a rare privilege, giving us the opportunity to hear stories of an exceptional moment in Oaxaca's history, and allowing us to meet so many wonderful people along the way, many of whom we are unable to name in these brief acknowledgements.

COLLABORATORS

This book is the result of the collaboration of members of the C.A.S.A. Collectives. C.A.S.A. (*Colectivos de Apoyo, Solidaridad y Acción* or Collectives for Support, Solidarity and Action) are centers for solidarity work in Oaxaca and Chiapas, México. C.A.S.A. facilitates the work of international activists as human rights observers, independent journalists and volunteers for grassroots organizations. For more information, see www.casacollective.org.

Editor
Diana Denham

Interviews, Transcriptions, Translations

Diana Denham	Chris Thomas
Laura Böök	Andrea Smith
Gerlaine Kiamco	Riccardo D'Emidio
Patrick Lincoln	Elizabeth O'Brien
Kate Benward	Silvia Hernández

Layout
Tim Gibbon
Diana Denham

Cover Design
Tim Gibbon

Cover Photo
Eleuterio García

See pages 372-375 for photo credits

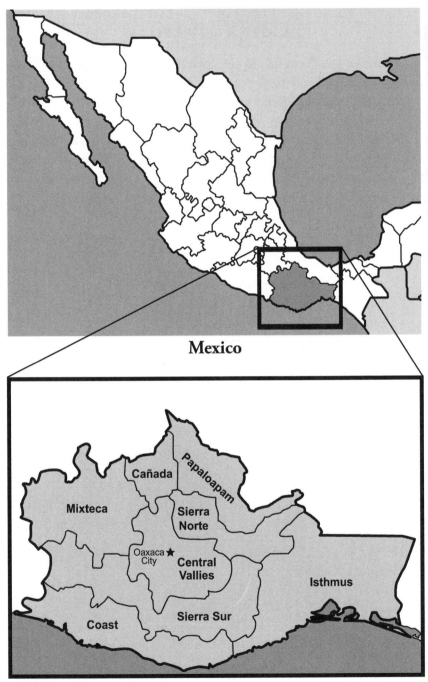

Mexico

Cañada

Papaloapam

Mixteca

Sierra
Norte

Oaxaca
City ★ Central
Vallies

Isthmus

Coast Sierra Sur

Oaxaca State

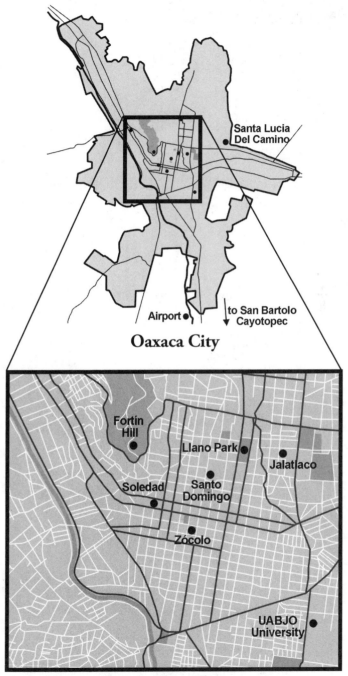

Oaxaca City

Oaxaca City Center

PREFACE

By Diana Denham and Laura Böök

It was July 2006, just one month after the police attack on striking teachers in Oaxaca, when we began to weave our way through the colorful plastic tarps that lined the streets. These makeshift tents sheltered a massive social movement that seemed to have formed almost overnight. The tens of thousands of people camped out in protest were reading newspapers, holding meetings, updating each other on the latest events...and sewing. As far as we could tell, the face of the revolution was a sea of embroidering women, patiently awaiting the resignation of their repressive governor. And we wondered, were these the urban guerrillas decried in the mainstream media? Despite the fact that armed attacks against protesters were organized by the government, it was movement participants who were constantly demonized as violent and menacing in state-run and commercial media.

A group of international activists, human rights observers, and volunteers for grassroots organizations, our collective hoped to learn as much as we could—from up close—about the uprising that had taken over a city and captured the attention of the nation. What we saw and lived would transform the way we understood movements for social justice in our own countries and connect us to the people of Oaxaca in ways we had never anticipated.

As the movement took hold across the city and beyond, state brutality continued while tactics of organized civil disobedience intensified in response. The social movement began to seize government buildings and organize alternative systems of self-governance. By the end of the summer, Oaxacans began to raise barricades in neighborhoods all over the city to defend themselves against attacks organized by the government. Late one Saturday night, we were walking back to the house in the occupied city when we got our first taste of community based self-defense. A fire was lit on our street, and a woman with a flashlight checked all the cars that lined up to pass. We stopped to talk with our neighbors standing guard. While some of the barricades around the city were made of cars, buses, or large stones, the one on our street had a more homemade look: bricks, wooden crates, a broken washing machine, a cardboard cut-out of a cactus that looked like it belonged in a high school play, a plastic skull. Someone brought us coffee and we stayed for awhile chatting—in the midst of their stories and laughter, our neighbors told us that they were prepared to risk their lives for what they believed in. *Radio Universidad* was on in the background, playing music to keep up the spirits of the people at the barricades. When it was time to head home that night, eight women from the barricade, all armed with baseball bats, escorted us down the street to our house to ensure that we got there safely.

Everyone could feel the tension rising. Glued to our radio during the entire month of October, we listened to the calls for peaceful resistance and reinforcement at the barricades under attack. At the end of October, there was an urgent knock at our door in the middle of the night; a friend arrived seeking refuge. He had been forced to run for his life when forty armed men in unmarked vehicles showed up and opened fire at a nearby barricade. All over Oaxaca, the same thing was happening.

By the end of the month, thousands of federal police troops had invaded the city and their helicopters circled low, stirring terror in all of us and dropping teargas at any confrontation. *Radio Universidad* urged people to go outside with mirrors to blind the helicopters, and we watched from our rooftop as our neighbors held up their mirrors each time the helicopters flew overhead. The valley below filled with shimmering light as people throughout the city did the same.

We watched as the invasion of federal police violently displaced the barricades and the *plantón* encampments, turning the once lively, colorful *zócalo* into a military base. Some bold people approached the rows of armed riot police, handing them flowers, reading passages from the Bible or waving the Mexican flag to remind them that they, too, are pueblo. "Your skin is dark like ours. You're being used to do the government's dirty work, but you're working class people just like us," we heard the people shout to the police. We watched as two young girls timidly approached the men with a can of paint. "Should we do it or not?" they seemed to whisper to each other before they began to paint the shields, one by one, to spell the word ASSASSINS.

An old woman who sold tamales nearby shared her disgust as President Vicente Fox appeared on television, thanking the federal police for restoring peace in Oaxaca. "Pero qué tipo de paz!? What kind of peace is this?" she asked us. Then she ran her latest idea by us as she spread salsa over another tamale: "I saw on TV how in Iraq they brought down a helicopter with a Molotov cocktail. Do you think someone could do that in Oaxaca?"

All of us who formed part of the collective had anti-authoritarian leanings—we knew the history of dirty wars, grasped repressive political-economic models, understood the consequences of monopolistic media control. But being aware of this kind of repression hadn't prepared us for the lived experience—how painful it was, how powerless we felt upon hearing about the arrests and torture of activists, the fear we felt for our friends.

By November 2nd twenty people had been killed and Day of the Dead, one of the most important religious holidays of the year, took on special significance. Defying the armed riot police just down the block, artists made murals in the streets from sand and colored chalk to commemorate the movement's dead. The most prominent church in Oaxaca, Santo Domingo, was framed by dozens of altars and the flickering light of their candles. These altars, each replete with marigolds, photos and favorite foods as offerings, honored *compañeros* fallen in the struggle. At the altar of the U.S. journalist who had been assassinated the previous Friday, an old woman asked us, "Do you know what Brad liked to drink?" A friend responded, "I think I once saw him having *mezcal.*" "Okay, I'll put a bottle of *mezcal* for him on his altar, then," the woman replied.

Later that month, on November 25, 2006, a brutal wave of police repression swept through the city. Nobody was safe—not protestors, not bystanders, not journalists. A group of independent journalists sought refuge at our house, and throughout the city people hid in safe houses as police and paramilitaries combed the streets and gunshots rang through the night.

On the following morning, the movement had vanished from the streets. *Radio Universidad* was silent. Instead, the infamous *Radio Ciudadana*, an illegally broadcasting, government-sponsored radio used to incite violence against people in the social movement, began naming addresses of houses that had supposedly given support to protestors. We heard that our house had been mentioned. That same day, an article in one of the national newspapers stated that the federal police were looking to deport a hundred foreigners. In light of the witch hunt that had begun, many of us left for Mexico City. Like so many of the testimonies in this book reveal, it is terrible to feel like a criminal on the run when you know you have done nothing wrong. Is it a crime to offer a safe place to a friend who fears he might be killed? Is it a crime to splash vinegar in the faces of people blinded and asphyxiated by teargas? Is it a crime to bear witness?

A few weeks later, things seemed to be calming down, and we were able to return to Oaxaca City, which had received a makeover for Christmas. The *zócalo*, which had been a military base for several months, showed hardly a sign of police presence and was instead filled with Christmas trees and poinsettias that bore cards written in crayons, as if from children, saying things like, "Thank you, federal police, for restoring peace in Oaxaca."

People were quietly reorganizing, considering strategies for the months to come, weighing options. Many were afraid to speak out just yet. Those of us who had just returned were wondering how to process all that we had witnessed, how to understand the experiences of the people so shaken by this movement that had gripped their lives.

***

This book comes out of months of informal conversations with Oaxacans dedicated to making change in their state. The testimonies were collected, transcribed and translated over the course of a year, and the process usually began at sit-ins, barricades or marches where we started to form friendships and build relationships of trust. The idea for compiling a book of testimonies formalized during the visit of a human rights delegation in December, just after we returned, and less than one month after the worst repression that Oaxaca had experienced. We heard testimony after testimony of illegal arrests, torture, and pleas for support. Pedro Matías, journalist for *Noticias*, whose testimony appears in this book, described the events of November 25th. He recounted the fear and the utter impotence he felt at seeing the people's demands for direct democracy met time and time again with violent repression. We watched as Pedro relived those moments as he spoke. He buried his face in his hands, sobbing, and paused again and again to compose himself.

Tears punctuated most of the stories we heard; the people who shared their testimonies were profoundly wounded. After Pedro spoke, we heard another account of that same day. Aurelia is a maid, who had not previously participated in the movement. Upon leaving the house where she worked, she found herself trapped in thick clouds of teargas, unable to walk or breathe. Disoriented and terrified, she was quickly surrounded by police, arrested, tortured and then flown to a high security prison in the north of the country.

There were also many people who managed to remain hopeful, vowing to continue organizing despite the hostile climate of repression. There were those who shared with us the triumphs of the movement. Leyla described how, in spite of the prevalent chauvinism and male-domination of political spaces, women carved out a place for themselves with the March of Pots and Pans and the subsequent takeover of the state-run television station. Not only were women the pillars of support on which the movement rested (it was women who, night after night, fed the people at the barricades, the *plantón* encampments, and other occupied public spaces), but now they were also protagonists in a way that no one could ignore.

From that human rights delegation, we started making contacts with other people we knew who had participated in the movement and in each interview a story unfolded—always accompanied by laughter and usually by tears, grounded in hope and courage and driven by anger at the continued injustice.

"Once you learn to speak, you don't want to be quiet anymore," Alfredo, an indigenous community radio activist, told us. When asked about the movement and the months of intense conflict, the people who bore witness to the events can hardly stop to catch their breath. In their stories, they capture the shifting atmosphere that could be felt on the streets—from fear to hope, weakness to strength. Talking to people about what they were experiencing was also a way for us to process the pain we felt. Our idea for compiling a book, though, came more from the desire to share the courage, aspirations, and sense of empowerment that we heard from people in the movement than from the desire to document state brutality.

This book is not a definitive assessment of the movement that took shape in Oaxaca in 2006, nor is it a comprehensive collection of the stories that people lived and carry with them. While we made an effort to represent a cross-section of Oaxacan society, to reflect both the diversity of actors and the diversity of their experiences, there are at least a million people who took to the streets and all of them lived things they had never imagined. Their buried fears, earned victories, suffered traumas, and sown dreams are the answers to why and how this movement organized as it did. These testimonies give voice to teachers and students, community radio activists and artists, religious leaders and union organizers, indigenous community members and people with no organizational affiliation. Each story highlights a distinct moment in the social movement and in the life of that individual; taken together they attempt to reconstruct the trajectory of events as they unfolded. From an 8-year old's struggle to free his father and other political prisoners to a great-grandmother who participated in the takeover of the state television station, these testimonies offer glimpses into the spirit of the resistance.

Introduction

By Diana Denham, Patrick Lincoln and Chris Thomas

Beginning in the spring of 2006, hundreds of thousands of Oaxacans have raised their voices against the abuses of the state government: grinding poverty, widespread human rights violations, and rampant government corruption. These mobilizations represent an unprecedented attempt to address the cultural, economic, social and political marginalization that has accompanied eighty years of single-party rule by the PRI. The broad and inclusive movement that emerged in May 2006 has captivated the nation and earned the admiration of communities organizing for social justice around the world.

On June 14, 2006, a massive state police force was deployed to Oaxaca City. Using clubs, teargas, firearms and helicopters, they displaced a sit-in of more than 20,000 teachers representing Oaxaca's historically combative section XXII of the National Union of Education Workers. The teachers had been occupying the city center for three weeks to demand a living wage, resources for infrastructure repair, and free schoolbooks and social services for poor students. This state-sponsored violence was the latest in a long history of government attempts to silence social movements. But this time, people decided to fight back. In an unprecedented response that the government never anticipated, the teachers regrouped and reclaimed the city center from the police, but not before the violence triggered a massive public outcry, from which the Popular Assembly of the Peoples of Oaxaca—the APPO—was born. State governor Ulises Ruiz Ortiz, widely believed to have come to power through fraudulent elections in 2004, had thrown a match into the tinderbox.

Marches in solidarity with the teachers flooded the city in the days following the June 14th attack. People from all over the state came out to help the teachers rebuild their *plantón* encampment and to offer food to those camped out in protest. The solidarity that came from virtually every sector of society stemmed not so much from outright support for the teachers' demands as from indignation at the use of state force against peaceful protestors and long-held desires for power to be dispersed among Oaxaca's many distinct indigenous communities. Three days after the initial attack, the APPO held its first statewide assembly, which was attended by representatives of 300 social organizations, student and activist collectives, as well as individuals who didn't belong to any organization. While focusing their energies on the demand everyone could agree upon—the resignation of the governor responsible for the repression—the APPO also started organizing for everything from institutional reform to regional autonomy. While the APPO took on a formal structure with a centralized leadership eventually susceptible to co-opting by a number of career politicians, it also became a powerful idea that gave name to a variety of actions and informal community groups. For months, the popular slogan "Todos Somos APPO"—"We are all APPO"—rang out in the streets with frequency.

Despite its spontaneous formation, the APPO—and society as a whole—quickly developed the organizational capacity to address the political violence plaguing Oaxacan society. These problems included the disregard for freedom of expression, the lack of transparency and consultation in the use of public funds, widespread corruption, a history of infiltration of indigenous self-governance structures and the ongoing repression of social movements.

However, in addition to responding to a police attack on striking teachers or a particularly repressive governor, the movement that surfaced in Oaxaca took over and ran an entire city for six months starting in June 2006. Government officials fled, police weren't present to maintain even the semblance of responding to social harm, and many of the government institutions and services that we depend on daily were shut down. Without relying on centralized organization, neighborhoods managed everything from public safety (crime rates actually went down dramatically during the course of the six months) to food distribution and transportation. People across the state began to question the established line of western thinking that says communities can't survive, much less thrive, without the intervention of a separate hierarchy caring for its needs. Oaxaca sent a compelling message to the world in 2006: the power we need is in our hands.

Behind the Flames

Despite its abundant natural resources, beautiful beaches, and booming tourism industry, Oaxaca is the second poorest state in Mexico with more than 73% of its population living in extreme poverty, unable to cover basic dietary needs. More than half of the state's population earns less than the national minimum wage of 45 pesos ($4.50 USD) per day. Only half of Oaxaca's 3.5 million inhabitants have access to basic services such as electricity and running water and fewer than 40% of Oaxacans have the opportunity to study beyond elementary school.

One of the most culturally diverse states in Mexico, Oaxaca is home to sixteen distinct indigenous ethnic groups, the majority of whom are disproportionately burdened with poverty. Corporate-led development projects have targeted communal lands rich with natural resources and biodiversity, dismantling indigenous peoples' rights to self-determination and ravaging their means of economic sustainability. While more than three-fourths of the population works in agriculture, the government provides no support for this sector of the economy. The total abandonment of family farmers together with exploitative trade agreements such as NAFTA also account for the extremely high rates of migration from Oaxaca to northern states and the U.S. It is estimated that 1.5 million Oaxacans are currently living in the U.S., and between 200,000 and 250,000 migrate north each year.

Such contradictions of shimmering wealth amidst the dull shade of widespread poverty and marginalization have led to periodic waves of social revolt. Unable and unwilling to address the root causes of social inequality, the PRI-dominated authoritarian state has long relied on repressive tactics to contain the popular dissent.

While more than 70 years of PRI rule came to an end when Vicente Fox won the presidency for the PAN party in 2000, the PRI has maintained its hegemony in Oaxaca through an intricate system of social and political domination. On one hand, media control and payoffs to local political bosses secure allegiance to the party, while on the other, intimidation, violence, and electoral fraud are employed to crush vocal opposition. Oaxaca's current ranking as number one in human rights abuses in Mexico is indicative of the increased repression of social organizing and criminalization of dissent in recent years.

Ulises Tightens His Grip

Ulises Ruiz Ortiz came to power in 2004 with a campaign slogan that boasted of his intention to smother democratic rights such as freedom of expression and association: "Ni marchas, ni plantones," he promised—no marches and no sit-ins. He moved the state legislature and government offices from the central plaza of the capital city to a small town outside the city in an effort to discourage citizens from holding protests in the center and to decrease public visibility of protests held in front of government offices. Despite evidence of fraud in an extremely close election, a federal tribunal with alleged links to Ruiz's party (PRI) declared him governor 15 days after the election.

When Ulises Ruiz took office at the end of 2004, the first thing he set out to do was eliminate the opposition. He immediately (though unsuccessfully) attempted to arrest Gabino Cué, his rival candidate in the gubernatorial election, under false charges. During his first year in office, there were at least fifteen politically motivated assassinations that were never explained, and over a hundred leaders of social movements were arrested throughout the state.

He continued the legacy of previous governor José Murat by threatening various opposition media including waging a continuous war on *Noticias*, the most widely read newspaper in the state. The government closed down *Noticias* stands, canceled publicity arrangements, and destroyed printing equipment. When these tactics were unsuccessful, the state hired agitators to pretend to be employees of the newspaper, seize the *Noticias* offices, and declare a strike.

Under the pretext of remodeling the city for tourism, and of course, without consulting citizens, Ulises Ruiz cut down old trees and replaced cobblestones with cement in public plazas all over the city. It is widely suspected that these so-called beautification projects were money-laundering fronts created to cover up the huge sums of money funneled into the 2006 presidential campaign of PRI candidate Roberto Madrazo.

In fact, despite the sums of money that Ulises Ruiz spent on the campaign, the presidential elections of July 2, 2006 saw the first defeat of a PRI candidate in Oaxaca in nearly eighty years. The center-left candidate of the Partido Revolucionario Democrático (PRD), Andrés Manuel Lopez Obrador, received an overwhelming victory in Oaxaca due in large part to the mobilization of the teachers' union and civil society against the PRI. However, right-wing PAN candidate Felipe Calderón officially won the nationwide vote by a slim margin.

This national electoral game played itself out on the battlefield of Oaxaca. Though the PRI candidate Roberto Madrazo came trailing behind in third place, he immediately threw his weight with the PAN, recognizing Felipe Calderón's victory despite accusations and evidence of fraud and national mobilizations for a full recount. The fact that the federal government, ruled by PAN, sent thousands of federal police troops to repress the movement in PRI-dominated Oaxaca several months later can be explained, in part, by the shaky ground on which Calderón's presidency rested and his consequent dependence on maintaining an allegiance with the PRI. At the same time, outgoing President Vicente Fox and incoming President Felipe Calderón, both of the PAN, were sending a strong message to citizens organizing nationally: social mobilization as a channel to demand attention to social grievances will not be tolerated, and in fact, will be met with severe repression.

Oaxaca Resists

The citizens of Oaxaca have employed widely diverse tactics

in their struggle to oust Ulises Ruiz and make their demands heard, including "mega-marches" of up to 800,000 people, the peaceful occupation of government buildings and television and radio stations, strikes, sit-ins, disruption of traffic with thousands of makeshift barricades throughout the city, public art, a 21-day hunger strike by members of the teachers' union, community self-defense—making use of sticks, rocks and Molotov cocktails—against police violence, and the use of public spaces to construct altars for assassinated activists.

No uniformed police were seen for months in the city of Oaxaca, but paramilitary forces terrorized public spaces occupied by protestors. These death squads, including many plainclothes police officers, sped through the city in unmarked vehicles, shooting at neighbors gathered at the barricades. The APPO, a peaceful movement that reserved its right to self-defense, responded by creating an alternative public security force called *topiles*, which responded to paramilitary attacks on people at *plantón* encampments and elsewhere in the city.

As attacks against occupied areas intensified, the movement came up with a new strategy for self-defense. Hundreds of neighborhood barricades were erected all over the city to serve as barriers to the now infamous death squads. The barricade quickly became more than just a place where communities gathered in self-defense; it was a space where neighbors got to know each other, shared ideas, and developed new strategies for organizing. The barricade was emblematic of the fundamental aims of the social movement to construct autonomy and direct democracy.

At the same time, the barricades also quickly took on a life and organization of their own, apart from and sometimes in direct conflict with formal APPO leadership. Barricade

coordinators were not from established organizations, and many came from backgrounds and experiences that had demonstrated for them the futility of electoral politics and negotiations with government officials. And while the movement commonly self-identified as "peaceful," with a popular and implicit acknowledgement of the need for self-defense from government attacks, the discourse of organizations in positions of influence with the government often developed a strategic (rather than moralistic) use of the word. More confrontational perspectives, often emerging directly from communities and barricades, were regularly isolated or written off as having come from police infiltrators. In this sense, the government was involved in creating an atmosphere of terror to encourage finger-pointing and paranoia, attempting to unweave the tighter social fabric that the barricades were taking steps towards creating. The same questions regarding centralized leadership versus autonomy that we find in movement-building efforts around the world were also apparent in Oaxaca—whether to depend on centralized decision-making bodies to organize mass movements or to emphasize communities in resistance that are connected to one another only through loose networks.

Non-profits involved in the social movement also organized a variety of gatherings with the purpose of creating concrete proposals for alternative forms of government. In the Citizens' Initiative for Dialogue towards Peace, Democracy, and Justice in Oaxaca, discussion groups were formed to talk about alternative education, economy in solidarity, cultural and natural heritage of Oaxaca, community media and social equality. Similarly, the Meeting of Indigenous Peoples, the National Assembly Against the Abuses of Plan Puebla Panamá, and the Forum for Democracy and Governance in Oaxaca were organized to generate proposals for alternative governance in favor of participatory democracy.

Double Talk at the Negotiation Table

In order to begin to grasp political realities that plague the state government, it is essential to first understand that in Oaxaca, separation of powers as mandated by the Constitution doesn't exist; there are no checks and balances. The legislative and judicial branches of government act as subordinates to the executive branch; the governor always has the final word. For that reason, the social movement has emphasized the role of civil disobedience to demand what they called the *desaparación de poderes*—a federal mandate for the resignation of the state governor. Oaxacan citizens seized government buildings all over the city, including the state legislature, and the offices of the governor and the attorney general in an effort to prove the government's inability to fulfill its responsibilities. The national congress would thereby be legally obligated to demand the resignation of the governor.

Negotiations between the APPO and the national Congress never achieved what Oaxacan citizens hoped. During the months that the APPO was at the negotiating table with Carlos Abascal, the Secretary of the Interior, the federal government was simultaneously sending elements of the federal police, army and navy forces to Oaxaca.

On October 19, 2006 the Senate approved a resolution stating that Oaxaca was experiencing grave instability and *ingobernabilidad*, meaning that the state government had shown itself incapable of governing Oaxaca. In other words, the Senate explicitly recognized that all the conditions existed to dissolve the regime and demand the resignation of the state governor. Despite these statements, however, the Senate never actually declared the state governor's illegitimacy. On the contrary, the governor maintained his position and authority. On October 28th, the federal government sent 4,500 federal police troops into Oaxaca. They attacked barricades all over the city and turned the historic central plaza of Oaxaca, the zócalo, into a military base, where the troops remained until mid-December.

Just weeks before sending in the federal police forces, Abascal had declared before Congress, "In the name of God, there will be no repression in Oaxaca." Understandably, the movement grew disenchanted with the negotiations as a result of the federal government's constant double-talk. They accused Abascal of holding the cross in his right hand and a club in his left, which is essentially the same metaphor used to describe the Spanish invasion of the Americas. For months, the APPO refused to negotiate.

Whose Media?

Besides addressing the lack of separation of powers among the executive, legislative and judicial branches of government, the

Oaxacan social movement also addressed what they called the fourth branch of government: the media. The state and commercial media served as a tool at the government's disposal to manipulate citizens and impose its hegemony.

Freedom of expression has been at the core of the struggle in Oaxaca. The radio station of the teachers' union, *Radio Plantón*, was destroyed by police in the June 14th attacks, but *Radio Universidad* immediately stepped in. Broadcasting legally from the occupied campus of Oaxaca's Autonomous Benito Juarez University (UABJO), it soon became the new voice of the movement.

In the now legendary March of Pots and Pans on August 1st, two thousand women peacefully took over the state television and radio station, and operated the channel for the next three weeks. When that television equipment was destroyed by state police in the middle of the night on August 21st, citizens once again demonstrated their resilience by seizing all eleven commercial radio stations in Oaxaca by the next morning. The APPO returned all but two of the radio stations by the next day, which they retained for the use the movement. Those stations immediately became the targets of constant threats, drive-by shootings, and signal interference.

On November 2, 2006, federal police attacked the university campus, home to *Radio Universidad*, using teargas shot from guns and dropped from helicopters as well as high-pressure cannons shooting water mixed with chemicals. In what turned into a seven-hour battle, neighbors, parents, students and other civilians took to the streets to defend the campus with stones and firecrackers, eventually managing to surround the police and force their retreat.

Cultural Resistance

Graffiti artists also played a central role in challenging government domination of the media, opening new spaces for expression by reclaiming every wall in the city for the people in resistance. New stencils, woodblock prints, and spray painted messages appeared each morning. Art collectives such as ASARO (Revolutionary Artists Assembly of Oaxaca) formed. These artists used their creativity and imagination to visually represent the marginalized, exploited and oppressed, as well as to promote anti-capitalist counterculture in Oaxaca.

The movement showed its capacity not only to organize political acts, but also to create cultural and artistic events to recover a history of Oaxaca unmediated by the sheen of tourism. The most notable cultural event that the APPO and the teachers' union organized was the People's Guelaguetza in July 2006, put on by movement participants and free of charge to the public. The commercial Guelaguetza, the most important tourist event of the year in the state, is a festival that celebrates folkloric music and dance from Oaxaca's seven regions. The APPO boycotted and blocked the commercial Guelaguetza, criticizing the festival as a Disneyland version of reality and an exploitation of indigenous culture, commodified and marketed by the state. Twenty thousand Oaxacans and tourists attended the People's Guelaguetza, which presented traditional dances from all over Oaxaca, including some that had never before been presented at the state-sponsored Guelaguetza. The success of the event in 2006 represented such a threat to the state government that in 2007, federal police and military were sent to block the entrance of the Guelaguetza stadium and attack those who attempted to use the stadium for the performance of the second People's

Guelaguetza. Forty people were arrested and many were brutally beaten in the police riot that erupted.

The Roots of Novelty

While the APPO represented a new and original approach to political organizing in Oaxaca, it also drew from forms of indigenous self-governance, known as *usos y costumbres*. The APPO, an assembly by name, emphasizes the input of a diverse body of people who discuss issues and make decisions collectively; similarly, in many indigenous communities in Oaxaca, the assembly is the basis for communal governance. The customs of *guelaguetza* (which actually refers to reciprocity or "the gift of giving") and *tequio* (collective, unpaid work for the benefit of the community) are the two traditions most deeply engrained in Oaxacan culture that literally fed the movement. In response to accusations that opposition political parties or "foreigners" were funding the movement, Oaxacans pointed to these customs. It was thousands of individual citizens, centered in the tradition of giving even in times of scarcity, who brought food to the *plantón* night after night for so many months, who set up first aid stands at marches, who gave away their blankets to people at the barricades. No political party, no rich donor could have even imagined the collective resources and labor that went into sustaining a social movement of such magnitude.

During all of November, thousands of federal police forces occupied the city center, further enraging citizens and provoking violence. On November 25th, in one of the APPO's many mega-marches, thousands of protestors marched into the city center and formed a ring around the occupying federal police forces. After a well-planned police attack, several hours of chaos and violence ensued, leaving nearly forty buildings ablaze. Hundreds were beaten, tortured, and arrested that day, and many movement activists and sympathizers not arrested were forced underground.

A week later, APPO spokespeople Flavio Sosa and Marcelino Coache fled Oaxaca, taking back roads through the mountains to Mexico City. The APPO had agreed to open talks again with the new federal government, now presided over by Felipe Calderón, who was sworn into office on December 1st. However, as a clear message to the APPO, and implicitly, to other organizers around the country, the APPO spokespeople were surrounded and arrested on their way to the meeting that that had been scheduled by the federal government. Sosa, Coache and two other members of the APPO were interrogated, tortured, and taken to high security prisons with charges of assault, sedition, and firebombing. Calderón's ascension to power amidst such brutal repression in Oaxaca seemed to foreshadow the way that he would preside over the country—supporting capital over human interests and only negotiating at the barrel of a gun.

When the government can only answer the demands of its people with brutal repression and propaganda campaigns to dismiss the legitimacy of their causes, social movements—not just in Oaxaca but throughout the country—are left with few viable means for change. As peaceful and legal means of achieving change in the country continue to be closed off, social and political movements are finding fewer and fewer ways to redress the grave economic and social problems that ravage their communities.

Numerous human rights commissions and organizations, including Amnesty International, the International Civil Commission for Human Rights Observation, the United Nations and the Mexican League of Human Rights, have condemned the grave violations. The Oaxacan government has hardly even paid lip service to these declarations. Instead, the principal reaction has been to invest in more propaganda. Television, radio, newspaper and billboards across the state are inundated with the smiling face of Ulises Ruiz appearing alongside public works projects for which he is supposedly responsible.

Evident in the immediately broad and diverse nature of the uprising sparked by the state attack on striking teachers, as well as the impressive staying-power of the movement, is the legacy of 500 years of resistance in Oaxaca. Beginning with Spanish colonization, the corresponding politics of genocide and the organizing that took root in indigenous communities to challenge that violence, Oaxacans have easily accessible memories of both the loss of and the potential for political, economic, cultural and social autonomy. The Mexican state, with the continued support of the United States, has historically acted as a racist, modernizing force, viewing indigenous lands and peoples as exploitable resources. Legal means of achieving change have, therefore, rarely been wholly embraced, and state power is frequently in limbo as a result. As a result of the state-sponsored dirty war seen in Oaxaca, armed uprising is left in the air as one of the options that many people would have never considered before.

While a Supreme Court Commission has been named to investigate the human rights abuses, Oaxacans have little faith that a real difference will trickle down. Despite the dead-end government redress, the air stirs with the force of a familiar slogan: "We will never be the same again." The city walls seem to share this same sentiment, planted in the post-repression graffiti: "Esta semilla germinará," from this seed we will grow.

ELEUTERIO

On May 22, 2006, 70,000 teachers declared a strike and occupied the streets of Oaxaca to hold a plantón, a peaceful sit-in, with demands for wage increases, infrastructure improvement in schools, and free books and school supplies for poor students. Rather than negotiating, the state government intervened with a massive state police operation, violently removing the teachers from the occupied historic center of the city with teargas, helicopters, and firearms. Hours later, however, the teachers were able to regroup and take back the city center from the police, this time accompanied by the overwhelming support of civil society and triggering one of the biggest and most inclusive social movements in Oaxaca's history. Eleuterio, an indigenous elementary school teacher from a mountain community in the Chinantla region, has participated in teachers' union sit-ins for nine years and was the leader of the delegation of teachers from his region during the violent eviction of June 14th.

I've been teaching primary school in the Chinantla, in the northern mountains of Oaxaca, for nine years. I teach in a community about an hour walk from my own, where the children speak a variant of Chinanteco that's different from the one spoken in my village.

Many of the children we teach come to school hungry. There are children who live in extreme poverty, whose families no longer plant corn and beans or who don't plant enough to last them the year. The village where I teach is just one face of the same economic crisis that has struck communities of family farmers all over Mexico. People buy their corn from *Conasupo* and live off meager welfare programs like *Procampo* or *Oportunidades*. It's all part of the neo-liberal economic model and the government's plan to create dependency instead of supporting production.

There are also children affected by family problems. Children who've been abandoned, children whose parents have migrated to the U.S. and never returned. Maybe they have enough to eat, but they have all kinds of other problems. And as a teacher, what can you do for them? You realize you can't do anything. If a child is thinking about her father who went North in search of work, how can you expect her to pay attention? If a child comes from a home where there wasn't enough food to go around, he's going to be thinking about food.

I used to tell the youth in my community that they should study harder. I told them they should make an effort to finish middle school, to finish high school. "But what's the point? Why should I study?" they'd ask me. "Then you can go to university," I'd tell them. "But if I go to university, can you help me get a job in my community?" they would ask. "Well, no," I conceded, "there are no jobs in our communities…" Then they would respond, "School's too difficult and my family doesn't have any money. No money for middle school, much less for high school or college. And even if I finish, there are no jobs. I may as well try to make my way to the United States to make a little money."

I teach first and second grade together, which is a mess because the curricula are very different. But in small schools in villages, the state hardly ever sends full-time teachers and the schools remain consistently understaffed. There are three other indigenous teachers at the school, but they're from other regions and only speak Zapoteco. I'm the only one who understands the Chinanteco that the children speak.

In Oaxaca, as in the rest of Mexico, there are two systems of education: the indigenous system and the general system. The general system could care less about indigenous cultures or languages and reflects the ongoing national effort to forget about the indigenous people in the name of progress. Originally, the state contracted what they euphemistically called "bilingual educators," but the objective was to teach children Spanish. In the trainings they would tell the teachers, "You're going to return to your community and forget that you speak a dialect, forbid that your dialect be spoken in the classroom." That's what they call our languages: dialects. It's pejorative; it's a lack of respect.

Later, people began to think differently. A whole movement began to promote authentic indigenous education. Not only should children learn to speak our languages, they should also learn to write them. But the general current in the government says that everything indigenous is backwards. If we keep being "*Indians*," the nation won't progress.

The quality of education in the state of Oaxaca is among the worst in Mexico. Every year, the teachers' union holds what we call a *plantón*, a peaceful sit-in in the central plaza of the state capital. The idea is to draw attention to the deficiencies in public education, our needs as teachers and the needs of our schools and our students. Thousands of teachers camp out in the city center until the government agrees to attend at least a part of our demands. Depending on the government's response, we may or may not decide to strike.

But in 2005, Governor Ulises Ruiz Ortiz came to power promising, "*ni marchas ni plantones*": no marches and no sit-ins. That is, he promised to put an end to Oaxaca's tradition of social protest.

The teachers' union is one of the strongest unions in Mexico and wasn't going to bow down. On May 22, 2006, we started the sit-in. As soon as we had announced it, the government began launching a smear campaign. On the radio, they would tell people, "Go out and buy anything you need, because the teachers are coming. Buy water. The prices of everything will go up once they're here." Or, "Don't let them into the city. Those teachers are a bunch of delinquents, a bunch of lazy drunks!" It just got worse and worse over the weeks. There was a bombardment of propaganda on the radio and on television, in all the media.

The main demand of the teachers' union was for wage increases, what we called re-zoning. A long time ago, Mexico was divided into three zones: northern, central, and southern, and teachers' salaries were determined supposedly according to the cost of living in each zone. In the southern zone, salaries are the lowest, but in Oaxaca the cost of living is extremely high. So our central demand was that teachers' salaries be adjusted according to the cost of living.

We also prioritized social demands. We wanted all schoolbooks to be free. We wanted children to have notebooks, pencils, and school supplies because all of that is part of the right to education, according to Article III of the Constitution. We also asked that school uniforms be free and that schoolchildren receive one pair of shoes per year.

Among the most important of the social demands was the demand for improved infrastructure. Many of the schools are in really appalling conditions. If there's a nail sticking out of a chair or a roof that leaks, how can we expect children to learn there?

The teachers also asked for doctors who would attend the children and for medical supplies in the clinics. There are communities where no one has ever been to a dentist. We demanded the most basic health services.

But Ulises refused to negotiate. He made an offer that didn't even come close to meeting the demand for re-zoning and said, "Do whatever you want, but that's all you get." Then he disappeared. When he realized we weren't going anywhere, that's when the media campaign really got awful. On the radio, they were urging people to burn down the encampment and lynch the teachers.

The *plantón* in 2006 was the longest in the history of Oaxaca. There are 70,000 of us in the teachers' union and at any given time, there were 30,000 or 40,000 teachers at the *plantón*. It was around June 10th when the rumor started to spread that the police were coming for us. The threat was imminent, but I didn't believe it. It was just before the presidential elections and I didn't think that violent repression would be the image that the PRI party would want to convey. It wouldn't look good for them.

***

The *plantón* looked like this: blue and red tarps strung up everywhere, over 64 blocks in the city center. At mid-day, the heat was suffocating. You felt like a tomato ripening in the greenhouse, but those plastic tarps were all we had to protect us from the sun and the rain.

Underneath the tarps teachers were sitting on the asphalt, on pieces of cardboard, on plastic chairs. There were backpacks strewn about over straw mats, cushions for sleeping, undergarments hanging out to dry. The teachers were reading newspapers or cheap magazines, planning lessons for when we returned to classes, playing chess or dominos, sewing and embroidering. I think in 2006, the female teachers perfected the art of embroidery. They made blouses, tablecloths, dresses for children, purses, hats, dishcloths, sweaters, all kinds of things, all embroidered with bright-colored thread. They could participate in all the meetings without ever missing a stitch.

Walking through the jungle of plastic tarps, you caught glimpses of all kinds of conversations, but mostly what you heard were teachers discussing the conflict, analyzing social problems, thinking about how to organize.

You could smell the perfume of women, the sweat of men who had been on guard all night, the aromas of food cooking on makeshift camp stoves.

It was the bright white light of the automatic streetlamps that announced the arrival of night, confused the darkness. That color came to represent fear for us because it was at night when we knew the police might come to attack.

But even so, we gathered together. Teachers brought their guitars and strummed love songs, music from the Mexican countryside, music from the Andes. We told jokes late into the night.

***

I was the leader of my delegation. On the night of the infamous June 14th, I told my colleagues: "Don't worry. Don't listen to the rumors. Get some sleep. There won't be any repression. It just wouldn't be politically strategic."

That night I went to bed reading Quijote. It was 3 o'clock in the morning when on the radio, we heard the broadcasters say, "The police are coming. We have very clear information that they're on their way. *Compañeros*, stay alert and be careful."

That was *Radio Plantón*, the only media that gave voice to the teachers. At every encampment throughout the *plantón*, the radio was always on. When the police came in, *Radio Plantón* was the first thing to be attacked, along with the Teachers' Union Building.

I saw that everyone around me was stuffing their blankets into their backpacks. You could hear noise, what sounded like bullets not too far off. I thought, "You've got to be kidding me."

I tried to calm down my colleagues, but people ran wherever they could. I saw tons of people running up the street where Alcalá intersects with Morelos. Then I could see smoke and my eyes started stinging like crazy. I had never seen anything like that before; I had no idea what it was. We could see the police shooting the gases. The shooting sounded like huge drums being struck: boom—boom—boom over and over again.

I tried to go up Alcalá but there was so much teargas my eyes burned. I walked ten or fifteen steps, but it felt like my heart would stop. It was the most terrible feeling, like I was dying. "What's happening to me?" I remember thinking. I could hardly breathe, and when I did, my insides burned.

I saw how teachers around me were covering their faces with their blankets, and I grabbed a pillow I had in my backpack to do the same. Some friends came up and threw water on me and the effects of the gases started to diminish a little. I could breathe a little bit and almost vomited. That much gas could kill people.

Half a block up, there were tanks and so many police. They were armed with high power weapons and they brought in dogs. We have bullets as evidence that they shot at people.

We started walking towards the park where there were a lot of teachers, maybe 500, already gathered. Thousands of teachers had been sleeping when the attack began: women with their children, pregnant women, and older people. We didn't know what to do. Should we run and get out of there as fast as we could? We were desperate, but we decided to stay to see what would happen.

People arrived from different organizations and told us that there were a lot of teachers who had sought refuge inside the Law School. We wanted to go, but the police were still there and the gases were unbearable. We knew we needed to organize, but how? Some people had gotten together some sticks and stones.

The *plantón* took up the entire *zócalo* and all the surrounding streets, too. The police invaded at all the intersections and concentrated in the *zócalo*. We stayed back at the Plaza la Bastida and people started bringing us stones and bricks.

I don't know if there was anyone really coordinating or taking charge or if it was just pure anger that guided us. I've never fought with anyone. I just don't have it in me. I suggested that we just leave for awhile and come back later, but there were a lot of people who wanted to fight back. There were so many of us. The teachers were as angry as they were scared and they wanted to fight back.

We approached the police and started throwing rocks because we didn't know what else to do.

By dawn, when there was enough light in the sky, I took out my camera and began to take photos. They said to me, "Come on, man, are you going to take pictures or throw rocks?" So I decided: half pictures, half rocks.

A group of teachers approached, announcing that nearby, they had a group of police surrounded. There were a lot of policemen spraying teargas from the rooftops of hotels, so we entered the hotels to surround them.

Early that morning, the helicopter arrived, dropping teargas canisters from above. The helicopter circled for at least two hours, but eventually it ran out of teargas. The government never imagined that we would resist for so long. We heard rumors that the police hadn't prepared very well for the operation, and that it was an error on the state's part.

Once the police realized they were out of teargas, they had to run for cover. I took photos of a police woman who had been hit by a lot of rocks and was seriously injured. There were a lot of stories like that, of police hurt from the rocks. They really had to run for it.

By midday, we had retaken the city center, this time backed by the outrage of Oaxacan citizens who came out immediately to show their support.

The police had destroyed everything we had in the encampments. They had burned a lot of the tarps, and they slashed through everything else. They even slashed my shirt, which I had left at the encampment. They tore up all the tents and bent the poles that were holding them up. They stole some things, too, wherever there was anything valuable. They really destroyed everything.

But people arrived with coffee and *atole*. They started replacing the tarps. They brought us lunch. The support was overwhelming. They said that we were right. The attitude towards the teachers that had been fabricated on TV—people knew for certain that it was all lies. We live in a country that's full of lies. The politicians lie, steal, and attack us.

***

Even if it seems like the deck is stacked against us, I believe we have to keep fighting for better education. We have to keep pushing the government to fulfill its responsibility to guarantee free education for everyone. At the same time, I think we can find hope in the theories of indigenous education. We, as indigenous teachers, need to value our own cultures and communities. Education has to be embedded in students' lived realities; local history and local culture should be the basis of the curriculum. The television epidemic has just the opposite effect. Children watch TV and begin to think that McDonald's is better, that whiteness is better, that everything foreign is better, and they don't learn to recognize the wealth of their own communities and cultures. The teachers' movement and the broader social movement that has developed are ultimately about autonomy and dignity. We can't stop fighting for the rights of the children we teach, and even if we are giving classes under a tree, we must turn the classroom into a space where education is made meaningful and relevant to the lives of the children we teach.

MARINITA

Following the June 14th attack on teachers, outraged citizens rose up in solidarity. Among them was Marinita, who is a great-grandmother and active in the Catholic Church.

Yo fui la primera rebelde. On June 14th, I was the first rebel—the first to rebel against the injustice.

I was born and raised in Oaxaca. I'm an authentic oaxaqueña. I was born in the neighborhood they call Dust and moved to Peñasco when I was seven. I am 77 years old. I have two children, eight grandchildren, and six great-grandchildren. All of us live in Oaxaca. I've suffered a lot of unjust things in my life. I used to work for the government and they exploited me.

Early in the morning on June 14th, I was sweeping the street outside my house when I saw my nephew, who is a teacher, come running towards me. His face was red and he was sweating. "What's happened to you?" I asked him. "They sent in the police," he said. When he told me, I dropped my broom right there on the sidewalk—because if there's one thing I can't stand, it's injustice.

I went all by myself, but I wasn't afraid. I have a lot of faith in God.

I dropped my broom and went down to the center, where you could see that everything was red. Really, terribly red. I hadn't come prepared. If I had thought about it, I would have brought water. They had used the most horrible gases. It was as if everything was burning.

It was 7:30 in the morning when I got to the corner of Garcia Vigil, near the Church of Carmen Alto. That's where I was when the helicopter passed overhead and dropped a canister of teargas. But God saved my life, because I had just turned the corner when they dropped the bomb right where I had been standing.

Around the corner, I saw the Chief of Police. I confronted him. "What is it you think you're doing with these teachers?" I asked.

I told the Chief of Police straight to his face, "You can't do this. Don't you know you just don't do things like this? What cowardice. You policemen are just a group of illiterates who have no idea what you're doing. Cowards!" I told him just like that. "Everything you're doing now, they're going to do all the same things to your own children. Remember me. Mark my words."

I was outraged. Imagine, you're just sleeping there and they attack you in the middle of the night shouting terrible things, "Get up, you son of a…" It's not right.

One of the police officers made a threatening gesture. "Oh, come on." I said, "You think I'm afraid of you? I'm not afraid."

I rushed back to the house and picked up one of my grand-daughters. "Let's go," I told her. "We're going to go and help the poor teachers, who are all crying from the gases and the fear." I went to buy water. I filled up a huge bag with bottles of water. I brought all that I could.

I was so angry at everything that had happened. I got so mad at Governor Ulises. He has no respect for the people of Oaxaca. He never asks us, "What do you all think if I do such and such?" He should ask us before he does things—whether it's destroying things, or doing things to benefit the people, or anything.

But he doesn't have the culture, the sophistication, or even the education that our parents give us. They teach us respect. And responsibility. If you have a responsibility, you should ful-fill it properly. And they teach us about empathy, how to put yourself in someone else's shoes.

In Oaxaca we pay taxes for everything. We work hard to

pay our taxes. All of us pay taxes, so all of us have paid for this. What a terrible misuse of resources. Doesn't it make you furious?

The teachers are fighting not just for themselves, but for the children. It's their responsibility. I've been to the schools in the mountains. My daughter-in-law works in the mountains, and she invited me for the Mother's Day party at the school. I saw the way those poor children walk to school barefoot over the hills. They come to school with aching feet and without having eaten because there's not enough food at home.

This man doesn't know how to govern. This is not what you would call governing.

This is the only social movement I have participated in, but I like to be active even though I'm old. I just can't sit still. If I have to be sitting down, I have my sewing that I can do. I've been restless like that since I was a little girl. I sing in choirs, and go to my reading club and my tai chi classes. I like to keep busy.

I belong to the Church of Soledad. I'm active in the Church, but I got so angry with the priest.

On June 14th, I met a teacher, such a humble, humble woman. She was crying. "Don't cry," I told her, "Be strong. Because God is in charge, it will all be okay. Let's go to my house and I'll make you a cup of coffee. Don't cry."

She told me that she had gone to the Church, she couldn't stand the fear. "The soldiers were chasing me," she told me. She had knocked on the door of the church. "I don't know who it was, the priest or someone else who answered the door, but I just cried to him, 'Please let me in, please. Open the door because it's terrible what's happening. Just let me inside the door, that's all.'"

But the priest refused.

When I went to the next church meeting, I scolded the priest. I said to him, "Father, I want to speak to you as a member of this church. Forgive me, but I have to speak my mind. I cannot accept what you did with a poor teacher seeking refuge here. It's terrible that someone comes to a church looking for support, for salvation, and is denied. She felt terrible—they were coming after her. And you told her you couldn't open the door."

"What does God say? Does God tell you to ignore your brothers and sisters? No, God tells you: love thy neighbor as thyself. To love your brothers and sisters who are in need. Forgive me, Father, but I can't accept this. If you want to ex-communicate me, so be it. But I have truth on my side." There were many shy women at that meeting who just stared at the floor as I spoke. But I had to speak.

There is a division in the Catholic Church. There are people who just do the things that are convenient, that suit them. People who close their doors to the teacher seeking refuge just because it's not in their interest to show any criticism of the government.

But there are others who have put themselves on the front-line for justice. The true priest is the one who defends the people, who defends peace. As for me, there are so many people who congratulate me, but there are other people who look the other way and won't even speak to me.

When the teachers re-took the *zócalo*, the people and the priest from the church in Ocotlán were the first to arrive to help. People from more churches started arriving, so I joined them to help. We started putting up the tents again.

We started the plantón again right then, and I thought, "If they get me, they get me," but with so much heart and faith in

God, I went on, fighting for justice. If I die, well, God knows that it was justice I died for. And if that's what He's chosen me for, so be it. Jesus came to the world to bring justice, and it was for justice he was killed.

At the plantón we started to meet *compañeros*, make friends, and form little groups. Every night we were with the teachers in the *zócalo*, and we would agree, "Ok, tomorrow, we'll meet at such and such place and such and such time." And we organized ourselves like that. I would bring coffee and others brought bread, or I would bring bread and others coffee. One night one of the women brought the most delicious tea, a pineapple tea. It was really delicious.

In our little group, there was a doctor, an architect, people from all different fields. We met each evening under the tents to share our bread and coffee. When we arrived, the teachers would be there studying or chatting about the situation, or reading. They shared information, "What are they doing now? What have you heard?" Things like that.

Now we're all APPO. They christened me APPO, if you can say it like that.

Later on, when all the attacks began, I never stopped listening to the radio. It was so nerve-racking. You would hear how someone had been killed or about somewhere that was under attack. Even at my age, I never slept. I couldn't always be at the barricades on my street but I always put up a little barricade on my rooftop.

I would go up to my rooftop every night and put up my littlebarricade that I made out of *ocote*, pine wood chips that I would burn. I could see out over the whole city. I had my bullhorn and would blow it to make sound like this: Oooooooooooo.

When the teachers were down in the barricades on those

59

streets below my house, I told them, "Don't worry, I'm going to help you out." So I blew my bullhorn whenever there was trouble. It's the instrument the *pueblos* traditionally used when they were being attacked. The attackers get distracted when they hear that kind of noise, and they know that there is support in the village, so then sometimes they're afraid to attack.

From my roof I could see the huge statue of Benito Juarez up on the hill. I said to him, "Juarez, come down from there. Come down to defend your people." I could swear that one night I saw him move down from his pedestal…On the rooftop, I just made noise with the bullhorn, but in the marches I screamed all kinds of things.

We had lots of little songs we would sing, "Everyone come out to see, come out to see, this isn't a government, it's a circus!" Or, "Whether he likes it or not, Ulises has to go!" I even shouted dirty things sometimes, like, "Ulises, go screw yourself!" I feel like another person at those marches. I can feel myself transform. That's how it happens. I can open my mouth and yell really loud.

I have some problems with my health. But God has put me in all of this. I can't tell you how good I feel in those moments when I'm there at the marches and at the plantón. I am filled with excitement, out there yelling and everything.

They've taken a lot of pictures of me. I even appeared in *La Jornada*. It was some time in June or July, after one of the marches, when everyone gathers around and has the opportunity to speak their mind on stage in the *zócalo*. I spoke. I said I didn't think it was right, what was happening. Brothers killing brothers. It's terrible to kill a brother, and we all share the same blood. That's what made an impression on the reporter from La Jornada. That we're all of the same blood—it's not as if some of us have blood that's blue, or pink, or green. It's all the same, so why are we fighting? The next day after the march, they had a little section in La Jornada where they quoted me.

I was there for the March of Pots and Pans too. We marched to the center and then—who knows where the idea came from—but we said, "Let's go take over Channel 9. The government's Channel 9!" When we got there, we kicked out the employees and took over.

I brought my little frying pan and my spoon and banged on the pan. I glued a picture onto the pan that I had cut out of the newspaper. It's a picture of former governor José Murat, the governor before Ulises, digging a grave, and a tombstone that says, "Freedom of Expression."

It's not okay to steal money. That's what I said on the television. I was on Channel 9 to say, "Why do you come and take the things that don't belong to you?" I denounced the government on the television. I denounced the abuses. On Channel 9 I said, "If only the Governor could come out to the streets and be with the people. I would even greet him, 'Hello Mr. Governor, it's been a pleasure meeting you, God be with you.'"

But many people would tell me, "Don't be silly. You know his only interest is in robbing money. He's only interested in stealing." The people hate him. Keeping himself in power by force—how ugly, how awful. This is a man without culture, without warmth, without humanity.

I was in Channel 9 for about eight days in total. I'd come and go. I have a little stand in Soledad and I had to be there, too. I sell key chains, cards, candles, rosaries, paintings of religious images, a little bit of everything. I've had that stand for twenty-three years. It's in the ice cream plaza, so whenever you want, just stop by and I'll treat you to an ice cream.

My children are scared for me. It's just that they love me. Everyone loves the little old granny, the mother hen of all those eggs. They say, "They're going to send someone to kill you. They'll put a bullet through you." But I tell them, "I don't care if it's two bullets." I've become fearless like that. God gave me life and He will take it away when it is His will. If I get killed, I'll be remembered as the old lady who fought the good fight, a heroine, even, who worked for peace. I tell my family, "There's nothing to be afraid of. God is with me." I've been in this struggle a full year now.

Hasta la victoria siempre. That's what I believe.

SARA

The human rights situation in Oaxaca remains critical. Since 2005, when Ulises Ruiz Ortiz took office, Oaxaca saw increasing violations of freedom of press and expression as well as freedom of assembly. There were more and more arrests of social movement leaders and increasing state-sponsored violence, culminating in the assault on protesting teachers. Sara, Communications Director of the Oaxacan Human Rights Network (RODH) witnessed the escalation of human rights violations in the months following the attack of June 14th, as an entire social movement organized to demand justice.

On the dawn of June 14, 2006, the state governor finally carried out the threat that he had held over the teachers' heads since the beginning of the month. The chaos and confusion in the hours that followed exposed the state's strategy to hide, minimize, and falsify the facts.

In the streets teachers searched for their colleagues. A helicopter launched teargas and the thickness of the gases in the city center made it impossible to breathe. Ambulances sped past on their way to hospitals. I, at least, couldn't believe what was happening; it was only fifteen days before the presidential elections.

It was amazing to witness the solidarity citizens showed. People came from all over to support the teachers. Around the city you could see how many first aid stands had popped up—nurses and doctors who came out to offer medical support. Many people came to share their food. At six o'clock the following morning, there were people handing out breakfast to anyone around; they gave me coffee and bread.

I was in the office most of the day on the 14th and the phone was ringing off the hook. People began to arrive early in the morning to report what was happening downtown. We had colleagues who were already in the *plantón* to monitor the human rights situation, and we were in constant contact to begin the documentation. Those of us in the office started making phone calls to hospitals so we could hear firsthand about what was happening and attempt to register the names of the wounded. At the end of the day, there were more than 150 reported injured. We monitored the radio, wrote press releases, and sent out the most current information available. I don't think we had a moment's rest that day.

In 2005, even before the violent eviction of the teachers, we could already foresee a serious political crisis and a downward spiral towards social instability. During Ulises Ruiz's first year in office, we witnessed the detention of community leaders, the repression of social movements, and attacks against human rights workers. We also saw acts of intimidation against journalists including the elaborately executed, systematic repression of the daily newspaper *Noticias*. The judicial institutions were not guaranteeing respect for human rights, and the State Commission on Human Rights, made up of governor-appointed PRI party loyalists, remained a silent accomplice to clear violations. All this has negatively impacted the state of civil, political, economic, social and cultural freedoms as well as rights of a collective nature, like the right to form a union and the rights of indigenous communities. The RODH produced several reports that warned of the deteriorating situation, including one about the violations of indigenous rights associated with the neoliberal development project *Plan Puebla Panamá*.

The operation created to violently displace the teachers clearly revealed the criminalization of the struggle for social justice and corresponding demands. Like never before in Oaxaca, public force was used against one of the most significant sectors of society. Everything that came later: the mega-marches, the six-month sit-in, known as the *plantón*, the APPO, the barricades, then the murders, the arrests, the armed aggression, violent displacements, and finally the invasion of the federal police, has all been the consequence of an authoritarian power that maintains itself at any cost.

The lack of institutional response to the demands of the communities and social sectors has brought about the active mobilization of civic associations and social organizations that work to defend those demands. The state has responded with selective repression.

The strategies of the state to falsify and minimize the facts varied and intensified over the months. The government used El Imparcial, a newspaper which consistently publishes government propaganda, to discredit the human rights reports that were coming out. They did everything they could to harm the reputation of *compañeros* in the civic associations who participated in the APPO by accusing them of being seditious and violent and by broadcasting false information about their personal lives over the radio.

Oaxaca's Attorney General, Lisbeth Caña Cadeza, insisted that this was a movement of urban guerrillas, while at the same time the administration was organizing what soon came to be known as death squads: truckloads of armed men who drove around intimidating and shooting at people at the barricades.

The state has done everything in its power to disparage political prisoners. Over the last year, the crimes that the arrested have been accused of have shifted somewhat. At first, people were largely accused of crimes against the state, such as sedition and sabotage; some were even accused of terrorism. For example, most of the people picked up on November 25th were sent to high security prisons in other states with those kinds of charges. Starting in 2007, people were being accused of common crimes such as robbery, rape, possession or distribution of drugs, sometimes even murder. We've seen a shift away from accusations associated with rebellion and a tendency towards discrediting social movement participants as delinquents and common criminals.

The impunity that prevails in Oaxaca is the result of a partial administration of justice, the politicization of the justice system, and the weak institutionalization of the state, whose control is based on the way the executive branch of government exercises power over both the judicial and legislative branches. There's no justice apparatus that we can trust.

So citizens organized to demand what they called "*desaparación de poderes*"; in this case, that the governor be forced to resign. It's a common expression used in municipalities in Oaxaca when a mayor or local authority doesn't fulfill his responsibilities to the citizens. If he misuses public resources, if he represses the people, citizens will organize to demand that he be declared illegitimate. That's what the social movement that developed after June 14th has demanded at the state level—that the governor be forced to resign. But that demand has proved impossible to achieve nationally, in part because of the contested presidential elections and shaky ground on which Calderón's presidency rests.

We can understand the Oaxacan situation in part by looking at what happened in Atenco. When Vicente Fox became the president in 2000, he wanted to build a huge airport in Atenco, a town near Mexico City. But the project was stopped because of the mobilization of the people of Atenco to protect their lands. That social mobilization represented the first blow to the Fox administration. And for civil society and social organizations it represented a great triumph. For Calderón, who took office in 2006, the APPO, like Atenco, represented the threat of a good example and the potential for a domino effect, in this case with the possibility of popular assemblies forming in states around Mexico. And if organized social mobilization can overthrow a governor, why not a president? That was more or less the logic that led Fox to send in the federal police troops to repress the movement at the end of his term and the reason that Calderón allowed the repression to continue and the demands to remain unresolved. The APPO suggested that a governor could be ousted through a mass mobilization of citizens. Obviously, he didn't want to pay that price and he kept Ulises in power in spite of everything. Social mobilization was not permitted as a channel to address or resolve social grievances.

Calderón originally used the pretext of federalism as his principal reasoning for not getting involved in Oaxaca. He said, "We can't intervene in Oaxaca's problems because states have autonomy; they have to resolve their own problems." But that only made the problems grow, until he apparently changed his mind and sent in the federal police troops to extinguish the movement.

***

If the Popular Assembly of the Peoples of Oaxaca—the APPO—has been one of the central actors during this process, the mobilization that occurred in Oaxaca extends far beyond. The movement also goes much deeper than the teachers' union's demand for wage increases, but rather synthesizes anger over decades of impunity and discontent amidst the incessant corruption and the enrichment of the local political class at the expense of the poorest people in the country.

Impunity remains a constant. Cases have been brought against the government officials responsible for the crimes against citizens, including the governor, the attorney general, and the chiefs of police, but those cases go nowhere because for all intents and purposes, the judges are the perpetrators. The state legislature we have is dominated by the PRI so you can bet that there won't be any kind of consequences for the responsible parties.

There are lawyers, such as those on the November 25th Committee for the Liberation of Political Prisoners, who are taking cases from the state courts to try them at the federal level, and even internationally, such as in the Inter-American court. None of that is particularly easy, but one thing we know is that we'll never find justice in Oaxaca where the judicial branch of government is entirely subordinate to the executive. It would seem that steps have been taken towards holding the guilty responsible for their crimes: a Supreme Court commission was named to investigate human rights violations in Oaxaca, Amnesty International has reported the gravity of the violations, even the European Union has addressed the situation.

All that, and nothing has happened. That's where our apprehension stems from. What is in store for Oaxaca? We are exhausting peaceful means of addressing and resolving the conflict. We've documented and publicized the abuses and we receive no response from the institutions. It feels as though our hands are tied.

I hope that the state government understands the consequences that are likely to come. The movement that has organized over the past year has been a peaceful one. There have been confrontations, but the people have been unarmed. We haven't seen anything like a guerilla movement. However, the risk is there. As people begin to recognize that institutionally and peacefully there is no chance of resolving the problem, and the government continues to close the doors on the possibility of dialogue, we are likely to see an increase in violence in the future. I don't know if such a peaceful movement will develop again, because people are very discouraged now.

Despite how disheartened people feel with the lack of concrete results that social mobilization has brought about a year later, the movement has succeeded in building awareness. One of the achievements of this movement has been to put the concept of human rights at the center of the debate. Before all this, who talked about human rights? No one. Despite the fact that the State Commission on Human Rights has remained completely silent, independent organizations have actively organized around popularizing the concept of human rights.

And as a defender of human rights, my role has been to maintain the ideal of human rights as a means to carefully observe the events in the city and to denounce the violations of people's dignity, especially those most directly affected: those who have been arrested, tortured, and the families of those who have been murdered or disappeared. Together with many others, our struggle is to return to the people their dignity, their humanity, their memory.

Marcos

The Popular Assembly of the Peoples of Oaxaca (APPO) was formed several days after the June 14th police attack on the protesting teachers. The APPO was created as a decision-making body with the purpose of initiating broad social transformation in Oaxaca. Unions, social organizations, indigenous communities, collectives, non-profits, neighborhood groups, students, women's groups, and citizens without organizational affiliation participated. The APPO quickly came to represent the common aspirations of the social movement and became a model assembly for citizens from other states in Mexico struggling against corrupt state governments. Marcos is the director of EDUCA, a non-profit founded in 1994 that works to strengthen citizen participation through rights education, grassroots economic development and support of autonomous governance in indigenous communities. Marcos was one of the founders of the APPO and has been active in the social movement by coordinating among non-profits and non-governmental organizations.

From the moment Ulises Ruiz Ortiz took office, his administration has been characterized by escalating human rights violations. One of his first acts as governor was to imprison dissenting social leaders and municipal authorities. He appointed the judicial advisor from his own party, the PRI, as president of the State Commission on Human Rights. He carried out policies without the consent of citizens and refused to dialogue with many social and political actors in Oaxaca. Ulises also did things that may not seem particularly consequential in the long run, but they represented serious offenses in terms of how a society views itself. He moved the existing Governor's Palace from the *zócalo* in the center to far outside the city in hopes of making protests less visible. Now the former Governor's Palace is a museum and a place that can be rented to the highest bidder for parties or weddings. Ulises also cut down the trees in the *zócalo* and "re-modeled" it without consulting citizens, who were infuriated at the assault on their historic center. Those are among what some might call "symbolic" offenses that gave fuel to the fire, in addition to a series of substantial abuses and rights violations.

EDUCA formed part of what we call the Collective for Democracy through which we made a series of reports in 2005 warning about the precarious human rights situation and increasingly authoritarian practices of the state government under Ulises Ruiz Ortiz. But Ulises' use of outright violence against the protesting teachers was the last straw for Oaxacan citizens.

On June 14th, along with many other organizations and individuals, we marched to the city center to denounce the repression. The idea to create a people's assembly emerged from that march. A statewide meeting, attended by at least 300 different organizations, was held three days later.

The Popular Assembly of the Peoples of Oaxaca—the APPO—was the Oaxacan people's response to the attack that the state government carried out against the teachers' union and other organizations who were accompanying their sit-in. But more than that, it was a question of injured dignity. Ulises came to power in 2005 through fraudulent elections, so there are many people who don't even recognize him as the legitimate governor. The APPO and the social movement that grew over the last year were merely expressions of a crisis that had been building for a long time, which the political powers haven't wanted to recognize. On one hand, we see increasing marginalization and on the other hand, we see people who are becoming more aware of the realities, who have gotten tired of so much deception.

So the APPO was formed to address the abuses and create an alternative. It was to be a space for discussion, reflection, analysis and action. We recognized that it shouldn't be just one organization, but rather a blanket coordinating body for many different groups. That is, not one ideology would prevail; we would focus on finding the common ground among diverse social actors. Students, teachers, anarchists, Marxists, church-goers—everyone was invited.

The APPO was born without a formal structure, but soon developed impressive organizational capacity. Decisions in the APPO are made by consensus within the general assembly, which was privileged as a decision-making body. In the first few weeks of our existence we created the APPO State Council. The council was originally composed of 260 people—approximately ten representatives from each of Oaxaca's seven regions and representatives from Oaxaca's urban neighborhoods and municipalities.

The Provisional Coordination was created to facilitate the operation of the APPO through different commissions. A variety of commissions were established: judicial, finance, communications, human rights, gender equity, defense of natural resources, and many more. Proposals are generated in smaller assemblies of each sector of the APPO and then brought to the general assembly where they are debated further or ratified.

The way the APPO was formed strikes me as something new, something creative, and at the same time borrows from the traditions of the indigenous communities, where decisions are made collectively, in assemblies. It allows for discussion, reflection and decision-making that happens horizontally rather than from the top down.

Since the APPO was originally formed, it has come to

refer to something much bigger than the actual council, than the actual APPO meetings. The assembly, which is collectively coordinated, turned into what you might call a movement of movements, insisting on plurality and diversity as fundamental elements. The APPO is when young people hold a meeting at the university. The APPO is when neighbors gather to organize their neighborhood. The APPO is the women who took over the television station. It became a fluid, dynamic space that allows for collective action and solidarity.

EDUCA was among the organizations that pushed for the formation of the APPO and represented the APPO in negotiations with the federal government. We have been active in disseminating information in rural communities about the experiences of the social movement in the city. Along with other nonprofits, EDUCA was also part of the NGO (non-governmental organization) sector of the APPO. We held biweekly meetings among the NGOs to discuss proposals and then presented those proposals in the APPO assemblies, and also brought the APPO discussions back to the NGO meetings. It was a very positive dynamic. The NGOs showed an impressive commitment to the social struggle.

The APPO has witnessed the astounding creativity of the people of Oaxaca to demand the resignation of the state governor and the creation of a new type of governance. To draw attention to the abuses of the state, the movement appropriated government communication centers, including television and radio, and held hunger strikes, sit-ins, and marches including a 500-kilometer march to Mexico City. Civil society also seized government offices, erected barricades, hosted open forums on alternative forms of governance emphasizing citizen participation, and coordinated cultural activities such as the People's

Guelaguetza. As violence escalated, people arranged for human rights accompaniment and the documentation of human rights abuses. We have seen an incredible capacity for social organizing and the construction of positive alternatives.

As the movement began to assume actions of greater importance, including more daring feats such as the takeovers of the radio stations, the state government began to execute a strategy of counterinsurgency. Imitating the practices of the APPO was one of the government's tactics. If the APPO painted political graffiti, the government made its own anti-APPO graffiti. If the APPO had radio stations, they made their own anti-APPO radio station. They used the internet, too, circulating emails that urged citizens to take poisoned food to the people who were at the sit-in. There were a whole series of strategies, obviously intended to harass us and carry out a type of calculated repression against us. Their principal tool was the radio: a government-sponsored, pirate radio station which they called *"Citizens' Radio."* What a name, eh?

The *Citizens' Radio* broadcasters began to harass organizations and individuals working with the APPO and in the social movement, especially focusing on anyone who had an active leadership role within the APPO. Since I was on the APPO council, elected in an assembly of NGOs, I was targeted.

Because my background is in liberation theology, they began to say that I had been part of a group of rebellious guerrilla priests and that I manipulated the bishop Bartolomé Carrazco, a bishop very close to the social movement and the poor.

That was one day. The next week, they were saying that I had a romantic relationship with a catechist and that both of us were hiding out in Carmen Alto Church making Molotov cocktails.

Then, right after the terrible repression of November 25th, the *Citizens' Radio* broadcasters begin to say that I was teaching university students how to make Molotov cocktails inside the offices of EDUCA. They gave the address of our office and gave a precise description, as if they were looking at a photograph. They asked listeners to come out to seize our offices and burn them down.

At first, since it was a more personal attack, I ignored it. But when they started to implicate EDUCA, it wasn't just directed at me anymore but now affected the security of everyone at the office. And since we knew the state government to be capable of anything—they had assassinated, disappeared, tortured and arrested so many by that point—we had to close the offices for a few days. Police—some uniformed, some not—began hanging around in front of our offices all day.

A lot of my colleagues would tell me over and over again, "Listen, you know there are arrest warrants out for everyone on the APPO Council. They'll pick you up any minute. It's better for you to stay on the move." So there was a period, during the height of the repression, when I was changing houses every day, constantly on the run. I even left Oaxaca for two or three weeks.

It was the most terrible sensation of impotence. All of us at EDUCA know that we've done nothing wrong, and yet the government does everything in its power to discredit the work we do. You want to say, "All I've done is express my ideas, which is a constitutional right! I have the right to protest and to express my ideas! What had I done to deserve to be in hiding—like a thief, a delinquent? Why do I have to escape the city like a criminal?" Our crime was to believe that we could change Oaxaca by participating, generating ideas, formulating proposals. For that they can release arrest warrants? How is that possible? But my colleagues knew that, with Ulises in power, it was possible-- that and much worse. The government was doing everything in its power to intimidate and repress the movement.

***

I really believed that Ulises would resign. The whole process of social mobilization was incredible; the movement kept getting bigger and bigger. But even with his resignation as a principal APPO demand, we have always recognized that more important than overthrowing a corrupt leader is creating the foundation for social transformation from the bottom up. Like the song from Chile says—I don't know if it was Victor Jara's lyrics or Violeta's—"Today isn't about the season of Allende's election, it's not about changing presidents-- it's about changing the country." The resignation of Ulises would simply generate better conditions for the process of social transformation, but it's not just about him stepping down; it's about changing Oaxaca.

The mainstream media heralded Flavio Sosa as our leader and people started to think that the APPO wanted to replace Ulises with Flavio. Even *compañeros* from other parts of Mexico asked us, "Isn't it true that you want Flavio Sosa as governor?" It was ridiculous. "This is not about leaders," we told them, "it's about grassroots social change."

The APPO thought it was necessary to create forums where people could discuss what was going on and formulate concrete proposals. The Citizens' Initiative for Dialogue for Peace, Democracy and Justice in Oaxaca included people from all sectors of the population: indigenous communities, businesspeople, Section XXII of the National Teachers' Union, the APPO, church members, academics, artists, and people from more than 200 civic associations. Through a series of meetings, they discussed and elaborated proposals towards resolving the crisis and creating the basis of a new kind of relationship between the government and society. During two weeks, these roundtables held meetings, open to all citizens, in order to formulate proposals for structural and political change. They worked primarily on issues of state development and towards the peaceful coexistence of the people of Oaxaca. Among these issues, the assembly focused on true political and institutional reform, a social economy, intercultural education, the right to healthcare, the right to free access to water, care for and enrichment of the historical, cultural and natural heritage, and the use of the media for the people.

EDUCA promoted this and other forums as spaces for reflection and analysis. Now, no one could say to us, "the APPO doesn't know what they want" or "the APPO just wants Flavio Sosa as governor." The APPO was not only marches, not only political graffiti; through the forums and the APPO assemblies, we had created an agenda for discussion and proposals that could be implemented towards a cultural, ecological, economic, and political transformation of Oaxaca.

At the beginning, we didn't imagine that this would be a battle that would take place largely in the streets. While my work, and the work of EDUCA, has focused largely on generating ideas for making social justice a reality in Oaxaca through these sorts of forums, we respect the expression of a struggle in the streets and recognize it as one of the paths towards the same end.

During the last few months of 2006, I was convinced that we were experiencing a historic, transcendental moment in the history of Oaxaca, and that finally we were going to see the fruits of our labors. There is no question that we were making history, but it seems now that this isn't even the first battle. The process of social struggle and organization has just begun and the political crisis only deepens as time goes on. As much as Ulises wants to say that everything is now calm and peaceful, there won't be peace in Oaxaca even if the APPO doesn't mobilize. Even if the formal APPO were to disappear altogether, the crisis would stay there quietly festering, boiling up from the bottom as long as the root issues were left unaddressed.

However, because of these events, these assemblies, the processes of discussion and reflection, I do believe that at least we have carved out our path. We know how to go about creating an agenda for change in Oaxaca. The APPO has taught us many important organizing lessons and about the logic of articulating an entire social movement. It's not enough to know that we want change; we have to know what kind of change we want and how to bring about that change. I believe we have created a rich space to continue reflecting on these issues, and these are the spaces that sustain movements in the long-run.

LEYLA

On July 26, 2006 thousands of people from the APPO seized government buildings around the city, including the House of Representatives and the Capitol. Leyla, a young activist from CODEP, which organizes communities in marginalized areas around Oaxaca, helped coordinate the takeover of the Finance Department and was among the women who first conceived the idea for the March of Pots and Pans.

"This office has been seized!" we shouted as we entered the Finance Department.

Some people didn't really know how to go about seizing a government office, but there were others of us who took the initiative. "*Órale pues,*" we said. "Let's go for it!" The force of the APPO at that time was so great that anything was possible.

The takeover of the Finance Department was part of the July 26th Offensive. We seized offices from the three branches of government: legislative, judicial and executive in order to paralyze the state and demonstrate its illegitimacy and ineptitude. A few days later, we took over what we called the fourth branch of the government—the media. Thousands participated in those takeovers.

The Finance Department was actually a pretty small takeover; it wasn't as important as the takeovers of the Capitol and the House of Representatives because it's not really a political center. But we did think that, at least symbolically, we would paralyze the economic functions of the government. The Finance Department is where revenues are, so we thought: let's get them where it hurts. If we're occupying this building, the state won't be able to pay its bills, and since the Finance Department is part of the state, it's a part of all the problems of corruption the movement is addressing.

There were only eight of us who seized the office. When we entered, the employees started laughing because there were more of them inside the office than there were of us. But even though we were only a handful of people, the movement had such incredible strength that when the employees asked us, "Who's claiming the takeover?" and we responded, "The APPO!", they all got up out of their seats and left the office, without protest.

Seizures of government offices have to be peaceful, political actions. They should not involve taking hostages or theft. At that time, the objective of the seizure was to make clear that work would not continue until our demands were addressed. It was an act of civil disobedience.

***

I'm 23 now and I've been working with CODEP—Committee in Defense of the Rights of the People—since I was 16. Ever since I was little I've looked around and wondered why things had to be this way. Why some people had to have so much more than others, why there has to be so much inequality.

CODEP has been working in Oaxaca twenty-five years, mainly in the Mixteca region and on the coast, but also in urban neighborhoods. We organize with communities towards autonomy and the construction of what we call *poder popular*, empowerment of the people, which we distinguish from the power of the rich. It's not power based on wealth, but rather on self-organization. The more communities organize themselves, the more powerful they become and the more capacity they have to create the kind of society they want.

We don't go into communities to give trainings. We don't, for example, go into a community and say, "I'm going

to teach, you're going to learn." Instead, we go to learn with and from the community. The knowledge base comes from the experiences of people in the community. We use the organizing structures present in indigenous communities: assemblies, consensus-based decision making, participation, and collective work projects called tequios. And all of what we do is based in respect for diversity.

***

Everybody participated in the takeovers of July 26th: teachers, students, people from social organizations, and people from neighborhoods and communities with no particular organizational affiliation. All the takeovers were peaceful, but sometimes we had to confront the police, who would shoot at us. So we had our *topiles*, which were sort of like the people's police. A lot of them were young people from indigenous communities.

At that time in Oaxaca, the *topiles* represented the people's police and the APPO represented the government. The empowerment of the people, what we had always worked for, was really happening.

After the initial takeover, more and more people arrived at the Finance Department. People came down from all of the different neighborhoods to support us. At night there were more than a hundred people there, including many women, who guarded the building around the clock.

We split into different roles and divided responsibilities by neighborhoods. For example, the Jardín neighborhood would cover the early morning shift, the Estrella neighborhood the afternoon shift, and Jalatlaco the night shift. We would sleep there until it was our turn to wake up and stand watch. People arrived from all over with food they had cooked for us. The *topiles* would come out to make sure everything was going OK.

There were threats of gunfire and intimidation at every government building that we occupied on July 26th, so we put up barricades in front of each building. At the Finance Department, we blocked off the entrance with garbage cans and stones. At night, we built bonfires, too. Fifty or a hundred people would come stand guard, which was a lot of people for such a little takeover.

It was in the Finance Department where we came up with the idea for the March of Pots and Pans. We were there chatting, and thought, why don't we women do a march where we symbolically close the hotels that were providing meeting places for Ulises' bureaucrats?

We made the banner, "*Cuando una mujer se avanza, no hay hombre que retroceda,*" when a woman advances, no man will be held back. In other words, we all move forward together. After that march, our slogan became famous. We encouraged women to bring out pots, pans, and eggs.

What a ruckus! Women of all ages came out. There were so many of us who showed up that we had to advance several blocks from the meeting place so that we could all fit. We could hardly stand the clanging of so many pots and pans.

We stopped at one of the hotels that rented meeting space to the House of Representatives. The eggs were symbolic, we hadn't intended for anyone to throw them. The idea was to show the hotel owners and the representatives that we had more *huevos* than they did, that we women had more balls. But our indignation was so great that we ended up throwing all the eggs against the hotel door.

We told the hotel owners, "You can't allow the bureaucrats to hold their meetings in the hotel. In doing so, we consider you accomplices. You're betraying the people."

All we had intended to do was close the hotels, but seeing how many people showed up, we said to each other, "*Compañeras*, there are so many of us here that we could do even more. Let's take over a radio!" Then some of the women said, "Let's go to Channel 9!" Not to take it over, just to ask for some airtime. But when they denied us airtime, that's when we ended up taking over the state television and radio station.

We went to the Teachers Union Hotel to tell the teachers what had happened, and that we were going to need them to help stand guard. At first when we entered, they didn't want to let us into the hotel. They asked us to identify ourselves. "The commission of women who have just taken over Channel 9!" we exclaimed. That's when everyone applauded and started cheering and congratulating us. Some of the men yelled, "These women have more balls than the Secretary General of the teachers' union, more than Rueda! *Vivan las mujeres!* Long live these women!" Everyone was so happy, they were crying from happiness.

I was assigned to be a broadcaster on the radio. "You're listening to 96.9, Pots and Pans Radio..." That's what we called the radio. There were only three of us as broadcasters at the beginning. We didn't sleep for those first few days while we organized everything. We had to broadcast first thing in the morning, supposedly to animate people, but we were so exhausted that we did it with our eyes half closed. Everyone wanted a chance to speak. People came from all over to send their greetings, to congratulate us, or to denounce the *priístas*. The radio gave so much strength to the movement.

The takeover of Channel 9 was really the straw that broke the camel's back; that's when the reprisals really began. The "death squads" seemed to have free reign of the city; they were filled with police in plainclothes who assaulted and terrified the communities. They made terrible threats and beat our *compañeros*. They even assassinated and disappeared people.

The people were outraged. Everyone was calling in to the radio constantly. "In the Reforma neighborhood, four trucks with ten men in each truck just drove past. They're armed and they're headed towards Radio Ley." Listeners came out to the streets to defend the radio. Their bravery was really impressive.

The worst day for me, personally, was the day they killed Pánfilo. Pánfilo Hernández was an elementary school teacher from Zimatlán, and the first teacher killed in the movement. He had a little corner store and always gave us a piece of fruit or something to drink when we held meetings in his neighborhood. He was so kind, welcoming, and had a way of raising people's spirits.

Pánfilo had just come back from the Teachers March to Mexico City. It was at the time when the Secretary General of the Teachers Union, Enrique Rueda Pacheco, began to betray the movement. Along with the FPR and some other organizations, he had signed the now infamous "truce" with the government. They were pushing to end the strike, for the teachers to return to classes. They were selling out the movement.

Pánfilo wanted the teachers to keep up the struggle. In the Jardín neighborhood meeting that evening, he spoke up. He said, "Rueda is a traitor. Why is it that the people have to end up with leaders like him, who betray us? I was in that great march to Mexico City, the march of teachers to demand justice in Oaxaca. I just got back. I saw the solidarity of the people, who

came out to the streets to support us." He said to the teachers, "How can we go back to classes? Let's do something about this situation, about this assassin." Pánfilo spoke so eloquently. He gave people strength.

There were maybe 100 or 150 of us in the meeting, mostly neighbors. We held it in a warehouse. We made some decisions, reached consensus over certain matters and people left the meeting in high spirits. Pánfilo had just left the meeting when we heard the sound of gunshots. I was at the door and ducked down and covered my head.

A friend carried his body to the car. Pánfilo's stomach had inflated, it was terrible to see. When we got to the hospital, he was already in critical condition. It was so awful. One moment, you have a *compañero* alive at your side, and the next moment he's dead. And the worst thing was, Rueda never said anything about it, never made a comment.

They held the funeral mass in the *zócalo*. So many people attended. It was terrible to see his daughter. She was fifteen. Her father had been killed right in front of their house. She and her mother wept inconsolably.

***

What I remember most about those days was how tired I was. No one slept because the worst attacks were during the night. I started broadcasting from Radio ORO after they destroyed the Channel 9 antennas. That's when the barricades began. I spent the morning at the radio, all day long at different neighborhood meetings and at night I was either at the barricades or broadcasting.

We realized that we had to have a way of blocking the

passage of the death squads, because they were all over the city. They weren't only attacking the radios and the occupations of government buildings anymore. They were terrorizing all of the neighborhoods.

The response of the people was amazing. The first night, when people said, "*Compañeros*, let's prevent these death squads from passing by putting obstacles in their way. Let's raise barricades." People took the initiative and started blocking the roads with stones, branches, cars, anything. The first night, they raised 500 barricades. The second night, 1000, and by the third night, there were 3000 barricades all over the city.

The barricades emerged as a form of self-defense, of pacifist resistance. They developed their own communication system, like fireworks as a danger warning. Some women even banged on their pots and pans to wake up their neighbors.

You found all kinds of people at the barricades. A lot of people tell us they met at the barricades. Even though they were neighbors, they didn't know each other before. They'll even say, "I didn't ever talk to my neighbor before because I didn't think I liked him, but now that we're at the barricade together, he's a *compañero*."

So the barricades weren't just traffic barriers, but became spaces where neighbors could chat and communities could meet. Barricades became a way that communities empowered themselves.

***

All of us in this movement have created a story that's very much our own and that shapes us all in turn. When we chat with other *compañeros*, we realize the similarities of the injustice, repression, and inequalities we have all experienced in every realm of life: at work, at home, at school. I've been marked by this kind of discrimination, especially discrimination against women. As women, we start to internalize the stereotypes society imposes on us from the time we're very small.

The most important thing is changing the power relations between oppressed and oppressor. These relationships exist on the smallest scale: within the family, within the neighborhood, and within the community. So the idea of "empowering people" starts from changing our own power relations and making them the most egalitarian possible.

Some people, when they talk about people's empowerment, talk specifically about taking over government institutions. We say, they may be right, that may be part of it, but if we don't transform power relations from the bottom up, we won't have gained anything.

CUAUTLI

For months, no uniformed police officers were seen in Oaxaca. No government body existed to respond to common crimes or work on behalf of public security. On the contrary, police officers employed by the state often appeared in plainclothes, shooting at civilians who were at the barricades or participating in marches. Topiles, a sort of people's police force, emerged as a response to the deteriorating public safety situation. Cuautli, a twenty-one year old medical student and APPO Council representative, formed part of this community defense group.

We were on the APPO Security Commission from the beginning. Actually, before the APPO was formed, we were doing security for the teachers' union plantón, as part of the POMO, the teacher's union police. We made our rounds: the plantón, the radio, the *zócalo*, taking shifts throughout the night to guarantee the teachers' safety throughout the historic center.

The *topiles*, the people's police that served the entire social movement, was formed as part of the APPO Security Commission. Traditionally, *topiles* are responsible for security in indigenous communities; it's a job that rotates among community members. In these communities, every man has to be a *topil* for at least a couple of years as part of his duty to the community. If there's a drunk or someone who's causing a lot of problems or bothering people, it's the *topil* who has to take care of the problem. It's part of *usos y costumbres*, which are indigenous systems of governance. So the APPO decided to re-claim that tradition and form our own security system, based in the customs of Oaxaca's pueblos.

The government had withdrawn all the state police, and they were training them to attack the social movement. We were basically like police, but police who served the people and replaced state police. As *topiles*, we were in charge of dealing with both common criminals as well as the thugs sent by Ulises Ruiz to attack the movement. There were about thirty of us, all young men, and most of us came from indigenous communities—from the Mixteca, the Central Valleys, the Sierra Norte, and some from the coast—that govern by *usos y costumbres*. Most of the *topiles* work in agriculture and carry machetes—not as weapons, but as tools. We come from communities where there are no businesses or industry; the work is mainly in the fields, planting and harvesting. A number of us came from CODEP which has a long history of organizing and has also been the target of a lot of government-sponsored repression. Also, we already had a political formation; we knew about government plans to exploit natural resources, we know how the neo-liberal system works.

Beyond the POMO and the *topiles*, neighborhood self-defense committees also came out of the APPO as another public security initiative. Each committee had its own structure, and different people in the neighborhood took different responsibilities: security, communication, and finances, for example. People in the neighborhood spoke about the state of the movement and the need to create this kind of organization to be able to defend ourselves. The idea was that it was people from that neighborhood themselves who were organizing to defend their neighborhood; it wasn't anyone from the outside, unknown to the community who was trying to impose control. The neighborhood committees had their own system of security. People carried whistles and firecrackers to alert people in the case of danger. For example, they shot off three firecrackers into the air when the barricade was under attack. Each barricade had a fire going, and the people at the barricade carried sticks or rocks to defend the barricade. By creating those committees and barricades, they not only protected neighbors, they also protected the plantón.

Whenever there were threats of attack people would call into *Radio Universidad*, which was our way of informing ourselves about what was going on all over the city, and as *topiles* we also called in with updates. *Radio Universidad* was our way of keeping ourselves informed about everything and also informing the population about what was going on.

***

As *topiles*, we would coordinate with the barricades. A lot of times, the neighbors asked us to help put up their barricades at night. They asked for tires or stones, or help moving things into the middle of the road. They would call us whenever there was any kind of danger. We were responsible for the safety of the people, basically. We maintained security throughout the plantón and made our nightly rounds to check on the barricades. There were a lot of nights we didn't sleep at all. There were a lot of thieves, common criminals, that we had to take care of as well. When they robbed people in the *zócalo*, we had to detain them.

For example, one time a storeowner was being assaulted while someone was trying to steal his car. The people from that neighborhood called us and we came out to detain him. He had taken a lot of drugs, too, so we tied him up in the gazebo in the *zócalo* where he spent the night. The next day we made him sweep and pick up garbage, and then we turned him over to the POMO. That's basically how it would work.

When we detained people, or when the neighborhood

self-defense committees turned people over to us, we tied their hands behind their backs and took them to the gazebo in the center of the *zócalo*. They had to stay there for a couple of hours, or else overnight if it was late, and the next day they had to do some kind of community service. Usually, they had to sweep the plantón or pick up garbage. It didn't really matter what they did, just that they did something. We never hurt anyone, but sometimes by the time they got to us, they'd been beaten up by the people in the neighborhood who were furious. The neighbors were especially angry because it was almost always poor people who were being robbed, not people with money. After a day, we turned them into the lawyers at the POMO offices, which were at the teachers' union offices. They weren't recognizing any government authority at that time, but there wasn't anywhere we could keep the criminals longer, so the POMO frequently turned them over to the Attorney General.

Obviously though, despite whatever proof there was, the Attorney General let them go immediately because the state government wanted to create an atmosphere of fear and instability. Also, some of the thugs doing the robbing and assaulting were paid by the government itself, so of course they let them go.

We also detained state police who were spying on people at the plantón and taking pictures. They were out of uniform and arrived at the plantón in unmarked vehicles.

At one point, we had considered creating a people's prison, because we didn't have anywhere to send common criminals. We were going to build the prison in Zaachila, which had installed an autonomous municipality. The idea was that it would emphasize rehabilitation. We would give workshops and prioritize the education of prisoners. People rot in the state prisons; they only focus on punishment and don't do any rehabilitation. The whole political climate was so intense then, though, that it was hard to get together the resources to get that kind of project off the ground.

***

Topiles were also really active in organizing the *brigadas móviles*, the takeovers of government offices. As *topiles*, we more or less directed the *brigadas móviles*. We had a lot of respect from the others participating in the takeovers. We seized small buses and arrived peacefully to close the offices, asking the workers to please leave. "We don't want any problems, we've come in good will," we told them. Then we'd close the doors of the office and paint, "This office is closed until Ulises Ruiz has left office."

Some of the worst attacks happened in front of the occupied buildings. We were guarding the Office of the Economy, when we realized that somewhere inside the building there was a group of people preparing to attack us. We knocked on the door and no one responded. Five minutes later, an armed group drove out from behind the building and started shooting at us. We tried to find cover, but we knew if we backed away, all the people at the barricade in front of the building—there must have been around forty people—would be in serious danger. So we decided to hold our position, and defended ourselves with rocks. They kept firing at us until their bullets ran out and they drove away, because they saw that we weren't going anywhere. Several of us were wounded. One guy took a bullet in his leg and the other got shot in the back. Later, some reinforcements arrived, but the hit men had already retreated.

We didn't have any guns. At the Office of the Economy, we defended ourselves with stones. As time went on and we found ourselves under attack by gunfire more and more frequently, we started making things to defend ourselves with: firecrackers, homemade bottle-rocket launchers, Molotov cocktails; all of us had something. And if we didn't have any of those things, we defended people with our bodies or bare hands.

Some of us had better luck than others. People in the neighborhoods took care of us if one of us was injured. We'd also take injured *compañeros* to the first aid center next to *Radio Universidad*. If it was absolutely necessary, which it was sometimes, we'd take a wounded *topil* to the hospital. There were several *compañeros*, 6 or 7 of the thirty of us, who were wounded by bullets, which were shot at close range from high caliber weapons.

Fortunately, of the *compañeros* attacked, they're all doing okay, they can walk, they have recovered more or less. On June 14th, one of our *compañeros* got hit in the face and hand with a teargas canister. His fingers were fractured and his lips split open. Two months later, though, he was with us again. Because, like the rest of us, he felt he had to do something with all that anger inside about what they're doing to our people.

***

Once you've been shot at once, you don't feel so shocked the second or the third time. I was in a lot of confrontations. On the night Brad Will was killed, there were attacks all over Oaxaca. We thought about going to that barricade, but since there were already a lot of reinforcements heading over there, we decided to head to the Attorney General's Office, which the teachers had seized in early October.

Everyone in front of the barricade was under attack. There were a lot of people there from the Mixteca region, which is where I'm from. In a confrontation that lasted about two or three hours, a *compañero* was shot in the leg by some masked men who got out of a car with a rifle and opened fire. Another *topil* was shot in the left arm. Luckily he was wearing a bulletproof vest that we had taken from one of the police officers we detained, but he'd been hit a number of times and was seriously wounded. A lot of teachers were kidnapped from the barricade at Santa Maria Coyotepec, and one teacher was killed and left in the middle of the highway.

There were already rumors that the federal police were surrounding the *zócalo*, and there were *topiles* who had to get out of town for a little while. Five of us were specifically targeted, so we each returned to our respective communities for a couple of weeks in October.

My family was supportive of my brother and me, even though they were worried about everything that was happening. My brother, who is 20, a year younger than me, was a *topil*, too, and both of us participated in *Radio Universidad*. Our parents helped the *topiles* by sending us a little money now and then, because they knew we didn't have any. Our family has always been active in social movements, and they've experienced the harassment and repression associated with working with social organizations.

I don't feel the threats quite as heavily right now, in part because I'm young and I'm not afraid. It doesn't matter if the cops pick me up. But at the same time, we have to take care of ourselves. There are other *compañeros* who were even more visible, and the police are constantly after them. Some of them can't stay in the city, because if they're seen anywhere, they'll be disappeared. They won't even be taken to prison, the government will just disappear them.

In spite of the harassment, and in spite of the fact that *compañeros* keep getting arrested, we'll keep working for social change and we're not going to let the movement die. We keep working in the neighborhoods, doing workshops and exchanging information about the conflict and new developments. I'm studying medicine, and as soon as I finish school, I'm going to serve the people, our *compañeros*, and provide medical services to communities that need them. I don't even care about staying in my town; I'll go anywhere there's a need.

EKATERINE

The Guelaguetza is the most important tourist event of the year in the city of Oaxaca. The festival, which includes traditional music and dance from Oaxaca's seven regions, is widely criticized as an exploitation of indigenous culture, which is commodified and marketed by a state that otherwise systematically marginalizes indigenous communities. In July 2006, the teachers' union and the APPO blocked and boycotted the commercial, state-sponsored Guelaguetza to thwart the huge profits the corrupt state government pockets each year. Ekaterine, a dancer and a student at one of the public high schools participating in the strike, describes her participation in the People's Guelaguetza, the alternative festival that the social movement put on, free and open to the public. This People's Guelaguetza was, for the first time in many years, consistent with the true meaning of the word guelaguetza in Zapoteco, which refers to the custom of reciprocity among the Oaxacan people.

By the time it was our turn to go on stage to dance the *Flor de Piña*, the famous Flower of the Pineapple dance of Tuxtepec, my feet were already aching.

The celebration of the People's Guelaguetza lasted three days: the 22nd, 23rd and 24th of July. The first day was the Great Invitation, called the *convite*. The performers went through all the neighborhoods of the city, inviting the public to attend the Guelaguetza. All along the way, people were giving away *mezcal*, the traditional drink of the state, from every region of Oaxaca.

The *calenda* took place on the second day, the day before the *mera mera fiesta*, the celebration of celebrations. The streets filled with people and the performers, with their huge papier-mâché puppets, danced with the people in the streets. I was in that colorful procession through the city streets, wearing the traditional dress of the "Oaxacan Chinas," Oaxacan women from the

Chinantla region, parading over the cobblestone streets in high heels. We went through all the neighborhoods in Oaxaca from Carmen Alto to the *zócalo* where they set off incredible fireworks in the shape of a castle and opened the *calenda* with a traditional dance from the isthmus.

We dressed in cotton blouses with lace on the collar and sleeves, tucked into bright-colored skirts—mine was yellow—and draped satin shawls around our shoulders. We wore our hair in two braids with ribbons woven into them, long dangly earrings and chain-link bracelets. We each placed a pendant near our hearts and carried huge baskets of flowers on our heads. You have to make a little hat for yourself so that the basket doesn't fall off.

With our high heels and those heavy baskets of flowers we had to carry on our heads, it felt like we were making some kind of religious penitence or a sacrifice to a saint or a God.

Those of us who were with las chinas, the women from the Chinanteco, threw candies. People from the Sierra threw coffee, bread, and turkey and people from the Isthmus threw bags filled with goodies from their region. Everyone throws traditional foods and treats from their region; it's *guelaguetza*, reciprocity.

The People's Guelaguetza came about because we blocked and boycotted the commercial Guelaguetza. The commercial Guelaguetza charges exorbitant prices and in the end, it's for tourists or the petit bourgeoisie (that is, the people with money) more than it is for the people of Oaxaca. The *calenda* of the commercial Guelaguetza only happens along the tourist walkway, not in the poor neighborhoods, and you have to pay a lot for a ticket to get into the auditorium on Fortín Hill where they hold the event. But where does the money go? The dancers are paid almost nothing. People know that a lot of the money generated by the commercial Guelaguetza goes straight into the pockets of politicians. We wanted a *fiesta* for our own people, one that real Oaxacans would be able to attend and enjoy.

We took the initiative to boycott and block the commercial Guelaguetza as a way of putting pressure on Governor Ulises Ruiz, since he hadn't responded to any of our demands. The boycott campaign lasted several weeks. One Saturday night, people from the movement went up to Fortín Hill, where the festival is held. They seized and blocked off the highway that leads to the hill. There were teachers at the huge staircase that leads up to the auditorium who were handing out flyers that explained the reasons for boycotting the commercial Guelaguetza, along with information about the People's Guelaguetza.

I stayed at the roadblock starting on Sunday. I was with the APPO security, on the road going towards the Hill. There were blockades from the streetlight to the auditorium and all around the Hill. The teachers at those roadblocks were mainly from the Central Valleys and the Coast, and each of the organizations that formed the APPO also sent people to sustain the boycott. At night we were really cold and a little afraid since there were constant rumors of a police attack or eviction, but nothing happened.

Some teachers painted "Ulises, Get Out of Oaxaca" and entered the auditorium as a symbol of protest. Inside the auditorium, there were things broken-- glass and parts of the stage-- but this damage wasn't done by us. Everyone was saying it was people from the government who had infiltrated the movement. They infiltrated in order to deface the movement, to discredit us as vandals. Sure there were acts of vandalism, but not by us.

After months of guaranteeing that the commercial Guelaguetza would go on as scheduled, Ulises cancelled the day before. Actually, he said it wasn't cancelled, just postponed for the security of tourists, and they didn't grant any refunds for those who had purchased their tickets in advance. The boycott had been successful and the teachers' union and the APPO decided to organize their own festival, the People's Guelaguetza.

***

I started to participate in the movement because my dad was a teacher, a member of Section XXII, the Teachers Union, and my mom is the leader of her delegation of teachers. My dad was there on June 14th when the police attacked the sit-in. At first I just went to the sit-in because it was the only way I could talk to my dad, since he was always there. Then I started to talk to other teachers about their experiences.

I started to understand the reality that exists here in Oaxaca, that many people and many communities have been forgotten by the government. I started visiting the communities. There are serious health problems and people who have to travel five or six hours to the nearest hospital, which is extremely expensive. There are children who go to school without breakfast, which makes them do poorly in school. When I started to see the situation, it made me feel like going out into the streets to defend their rights, to stand up for the people who really are forgotten. The government acts as if these people didn't exist, as if they weren't a part of us.

I got involved in *Radio Universidad* first. I was in my last year of high school, I was 17, but my school was on strike so I had time to get involved in the movement. At *Radio Universidad*, I answered the phone. I took all the calls: people congratulating us, questions about the movement, and the threats too. I also helped in the kitchen.

I had experience as a dancer because I had actually been practicing for the *Flor de Piña* for the commercial Guelaguetza in 2005. Some of the dancers from the commercial Guelaguetza decided to join the People's Guelaguetza and the other dancers they found by putting up invitations at schools. In the *Flor de Piña*, some were daughters of teachers from Tuxtepec and others were students who had seen invitations at their schools. Even though I live in the city, I danced this traditional dance from Tuxtepec because that's where my dad is from. The only requirement was that you had to be 15 years old or older. The organizers held try-outs and made selections. Those who didn't end up dancing supported the performance in other ways. A lot of the support for the dancers in Tuxtepec came from the teachers' union. They gave us a place where we could eat breakfast, take a shower and have dinner.

In school most of us learn the traditional dances. In elementary school, they teach you a dance for Mother's Day and in high school we have dance courses, too, so I also know Lu Poca, Jarabe Mixe, Jarabe Mixteco, Pinotepa and a little bit of Yalalag.

We rehearsed for the *Flor de Piña* for a week from 7am until 2pm. Then we had an hour to eat and started practicing again until 8pm.

The *Flor de Piña* is somewhat difficult because you don't dance as couples. Your partner is a woman who dances opposite you, and everything has to be exactly synchronized. The dance is all women. First we form two lines, then a semicircle, always in step with our partners. All the women dancing are holding pineapples, and the accompanying music is played by a brass band.

On the morning of the Guelaguetza, we had a dress rehearsal at 5 o'clock in the morning. In our delegation from Tuxtepec, we had fifty dancers and about a hundred people in total with the teachers and parents who came with us to the city to help with our outfits and everything. When we entered the stadium at the Technology Institute, where the event was held this year, all the other delegations were already there and started applauding, saying how beautiful we looked.

There were so many dances in the Guelaguetza from each of Oaxaca's seven regions. The isthmus presented the *Jarabe Mixe*, *El Torito Serrano* and the *Feather Dance, Danza de la Pluma*. The Pinotepa describes the beauty of women; the Ejutla is a song to a serpent. Some music has lyrics in Zapoteco and is more ritualistic while other dances are accompanied by brass band music.

People came from communities to present dances that had never been seen before in the commercial Guelaguetza. That was the big difference between the People's Guelaguetza and the commercial Guelaguetza. This time the people who came to dance were really from the pueblos, from the indigenous communities. You could see their roots and see that they were from the places they represented.

We danced wearing our *huipiles,* the traditional colorfully embroidered dresses, with our hair in two braids tied with ribbons and dangly earrings, bright colored beaded necklaces, and *guaraches*, simple leather sandals. And of course, the pineapples added the special touch.

The stadium was packed. There were so many people there, some were left standing. It was the first time that anyone had boycotted the Guelaguetza and held their own. We never wanted to cancel the *fiesta*; we only asked that it be for the people of Oaxaca. We wanted a festival where the pueblo could really participate, and where there was no entrance fee, and that's what we made happen. We made it a *fiesta* that truly belonged to the people.

The Guelaguetza more than anything is an exchange, a day of sharing, and the biggest *fiesta* in Oaxaca where everyone shares something from their region. In indigenous communities, the word guelaguetza refers to an exchange. I ask you to donate something for a party I'm giving in the community and then I return the favor when you need it. This is how the *pueblos* understand the meaning of guelaguetza. It's the traditional symbol of the Guelaguetza, reciprocity: to help others, exchange things.

I loved dancing in the Guelaguetza because you're with your people and really doing something for them. They admire the way you dance, and more than anything, it's the satisfaction of seeing how happy people are, how thankful. You dance for them and create something special, you give them that moment. There are many people who don't have money to see a movie at the theater or to go out for an ice cream, but everyone could come to the Guelaguetza. I think how much work we had put into it, how much care, really shone through to people.

I'm going to start rehearsals for this year's People's Guelaguetza as soon as classes are out. I think it will be even better than last year's because we have more time to rehearse and to collect donations of pineapples and bananas that we bring to give away at the festival. We'll boycott the commercial Guelaguetza again, and ours will be free to the public. I hope that the People's Guelaguetza keeps getting better each year because it is truly a *fiesta* of the people.

The Guelaguetza Popular 2007 was met with severe state repression in which 62 people were arrested and beaten and one man was left permanently paralyzed.

Genoveva

Since 1996, Loxicha has been the site of low-intensity warfare in which the Mexican Army, as well as state and federal police forces, have collaborated with corrupt local political bosses and paramilitary groups to target the people of the region. During the years prior to the army invasion, the communities of Loxicha had organized and succeeded in overthrowing the caciques, or local political bosses, who had robbed and exploited them for so many years. But in 1996, the government sent in the military under the pretext of an alleged People's Revolutionary Army (EPR) presence, and replaced the community-elected authorities with the same corrupt cacique system that had existed before. All community leaders and people who had organized against the caciques were arrested and tortured. In 1997, the women of Loxicha organized a plantón, a sit-in in the zócalo of Oaxaca City that would last for the next four years. The women demanded the release of their imprisoned brothers, fathers and husbands. Genoveva, 27 years old, left Loxicha to participate in the women's plantón and to work to support her family. She continues to be active in the Oaxacan social movement as part of the Oaxacan Women's Coordinating Body (COMO), working especially to demand the release of one remaining female political prisoner from the region, Isabel Amarez.

It was June of 1996. I had just returned to my community after finishing middle school in San Agustin Loxicha. Near the end of the month, at eight o'clock in the morning, about 50 members of the judicial police and Mexican military arrived at my house, asking for the name of my father and my brothers. I asked them what they wanted with my father and one of them responded, "Girl, don't ask questions because your father knows very well what he's been up to. Tell your father that we'll be back soon with a surprise." Eight days later they returned at midnight, kicking

119

the door in. They beat one of my sisters-in-law with a machete. She was three months pregnant and four days later she had a miscarriage. They couldn't find my father so they left again.

They returned six days later at about four in the morning, breaking down the door to the house and destroying everything we owned. They pulled me by the hair and took me outside. I told them that my father was not a criminal and asked them why they were looking for him like this, and they started hitting me in the face and stomach with their guns. They held a pistol to my head and threatened to kill me if I didn't tell them where my father was.

The last time they came, it was around two in the morning. They tried to rape one of my sisters since they couldn't find any of the men in my family who they were looking for. They robbed us of everything we had in the house, which was only five liters of gas and about 200 kilos of corn that sustained our family. Then they left as if nothing had happened.

***

On August 29, 1996, I was listening to the radio, which reported that a group of armed people called the Ejército Popular Revolucionario (EPR), the People's Revolutionary Army, had attacked a police and marine installation in Huatulco, Oaxaca. According to an official proclamation by the State Justice Department, it appeared that a person from San Agustin Loxicha was among those who had died during the confrontation between the armed group and the police. This served as a pretext for the military and the state and federal police to enter our region, Loxicha, on September 25, 1996. They began accusing indigenous people, poor farmers, and teachers from the region of being members of the armed group. The government then used the presumed presence of the EPR as an excuse to arrest all the community authorities that we had chosen in order install a new government made up of *caciques*: corrupt, self-interested local leaders who served the interests of the state government and the PRI, and not those of the people of the region.

Police and military checkpoints were installed at all entrance and exit points in the region. Day and night, police and military cars came and went with captured prisoners, their hands tied and faces covered with blood. We saw all these atrocities, but we didn't have the power to say anything.

My father is a poor farmer. He grows corn and beans on a small farm. My father and brothers decided to go up to the farm to work despite everything that was happening in the region because they thought that the farm was remote enough that the police and army would never come there. It's a three-hour walk from town and there are no cars or lights. Nevertheless, on June 7, 1997, around four in the morning, the military and police entered the small ranch while they slept.

That morning, 200 or more soldiers and officers surrounded the house, hiding around the mountainside. They were armed, uniformed, and some wore scarves covering their faces. Civilians from the community, who covered their faces to avoid being recognized, accompanied the soldiers. They were paid 200 or 300 pesos to identify houses and people. The soldiers arrested my father, Ponciano, and my two brothers, Celso and Alfredo. The police and soldiers tortured them before making them walk the three hours to the highway, where they took them away in cars.

***

Since the 1980's, the community has been organizing against the *caciques*, the corrupt local leaders who had all the power but never prioritized the needs of the communities. There are several marginalized communities in the southern mountains of Oaxaca that form the region we call Loxicha. All of us are Zapotecos and speak Zapoteco. Almost all of us are farmers, living off of the corn and beans we plant.

There is no clean drinking water, no electricity, no clinic and only one secondary school, but it's a 3-hour walk from my house. There are what they call "health centers", but there are no doctors and no medical supplies. People hardly have enough to eat. When a family uses up their year's worth of corn harvest, we're forced to buy corn, which is incredibly expensive for us. And now we can't even farm our land freely because people are afraid of the military presence.

My father and brothers actively fought for the community by participating in meetings and marches. From 1985 until the military arrived, the communities succeeded in electing our own leaders, but then the military re-installed the corrupt *cacique* system. My father has always participated in the community assemblies and spoken against the *caciques* who seek benefits only for themselves, so when the military arrived, the *caciques* identified my father.

My dad was in jail for a year and a half before he was released due to insufficient evidence. Though my brothers were less prominent in our community than my father, they were tortured and punished much more severely.

The State Commission on Human Rights has photo evidence of their torture. The first time they went to see one of my brothers they didn't recognize him, because his face was so swollen and bloody. He had been urinating blood and vomiting.

His ear was severely bleeding from having had an object forced into it.

Both of my brothers were sentenced to thirty years in jail for a homicide they did not commit. After three years, they were released based on an amnesty law created by ex-governor José Murat. This law promised the conditional release of prisoners if they accepted full responsibility for their crimes. However, this was simply another form of coercion and entrapment; even though they were out of jail, my brothers couldn't go about freely in their communities, and if they protested against any mistreatment, they would be arrested again. My brothers are afraid to pursue their cases because it's the people from the government who are the very ones who had them captured and tortured in the first place and because the military and paramilitary presence remains strong in our community.

People in Loxicha are organizing for the right to choose our own leaders, even though the intimidation and harassment continues. Today the mayor is a supporter of Governor Ulises Ruiz Ortiz.

The government has never been able to prove that the EPR even exists in Loxicha. We wonder how armed groups could exist there when we don't even have enough to eat, much less money to buy weapons. We're not a part of any armed group. We respect different forms of social struggle, but ours has always been peaceful. We don't believe in armed struggle.

***

All political prisoners face threats and torture. If they don't confess guilt, the police threaten to kill them and their families. Confessions are obtained without the presence of a lawyer and oftentimes the prisoner doesn't even speak Spanish.

The state threatened and intimidated our prisoners in the same way they have threatened social activists more recently in Oaxaca City. The political prisoners are forced to sign blank documents on which the police can later write whatever false confession they choose. The police transport them to the prisons in helicopters and threaten to throw them overboard. They threaten to harm their families. Those are all things that they did to my brothers.

The time that my dad and brothers were in jail was difficult for my family. My mom stayed in the community and I had to relocate to the city in order to help support my seven brothers and sisters and be with my *compañeras* in the *plantón*; we set up a permanent sit-in in the *zócalo* to demand the release of our political prisoners and an end to the repression. My mom had to ask for loans from people in the community to buy corn. My family is still paying off the debts to this day.

***

Now I'm working in the city selling bus tickets at the second class bus station. I couldn't finish high school because I had come to the city to escape the repression and to work to help my family. The only cash that comes into the community is from selling fifty or sixty kilos of coffee beans per year, but that only brings in a tiny bit of money. I used to work from 6am to 11pm, but when I found out that the Oaxacan Women's Coordinating Body (COMO), the biggest women's organization within the APPO, had reopened the case of Isabel Armaraz Matias, I started working part time in order to support the COMO. Isabel Aramaz is a *compañera* from my community who had fought with us and who has now been in jail for more than five years. Along with the many demands of the APPO and a demand for special attention to the rights of women, a principal demand of the COMO is the release of Isabel. Isabel, who is one of the remaining political prisoners from my region who has been in jail for more than five years, is one of the main reasons I've dedicated so much to the COMO.

Isabel is an indigenous Zapotec from the Loma Bonita Loxicha community in the Sierra Sur. She was a housewife who was always active in her community; she participated in the march from Oaxaca City to Mexico City in 1992, demanding the release of Dr. Felipe Martínez Soriano. During the repression of 1996, the army, police and paramilitaries known as *entregadores* persecuted Isabel and her family. She and her husband made the decision to leave the community and relocate to the city in order to look for work and a way to survive since paramilitaries kept them under surveillance day and night. Her mother and father, along with her sisters, stayed in their community. Months later, her father was kidnapped and held by the police for 24 hours.

Around noon on June 25, 2002, Isabel and her daughters left the civil hospital in Oaxaca City where the doctors had told Isabel that her mother was very ill and in a coma. She decided to get some rest and clean her house while her sisters attended to their mother. When she entered her house with her daughters, shots were fired from outside and bullets entered all parts of the house. The only thing that she could do was hold her daughters and try to hide. She didn't understand what was happening. They pulled her daughters out of her arms and handcuffed her. They drove Isabel to an office where they interrogated her. When she asked why they were arresting her, they told her, "You kidnapped a young boy and are part of the People's Revolutionary

Army." They told her that if she didn't confess they would take her daughters away from her. They beat her all over her body and forced her to sign blank documents.

After the interrogation, they moved her to Santa María Ixcotel prison. She never got a chance to make a phone call, not even to ask about the health of her mother. After four months of incarceration, Isabel received the terrible news that her mother had died in the hospital. Desperate, she asked prison authorities if they would give her the opportunity to say goodbye to her mother, but they never gave her that chance.

Isabel is a social activist from my community, so for that reason, I felt the need to join the people's movement that emerged over the past year in Oaxaca City, specifically the organizations within the movement that defend the rights of women. Of course, I also decided to participate because of everything I have lived through personally and for all that our communities have been forced to endure: the repression, assassinations, forced disappearances and wrongful imprisonments. We've suffered so much at the hands of the state government.

It's been ten years since I lived peacefully in my house with my family. How many more years must I wait to live in dignity with my loved ones?

For a long time, women didn't have a voice or a vote in the communities; the men decided everything. But today, spaces are opening up for women little by little. Women are included in meetings, participate in discussions, and are allowed to vote. Things are changing because of everything we have been fighting for since the repression of 1996-1997, when we, as women and family members of political prisoners, saw the necessity to take action.

Women began relocating to the city to denounce what was

taking place. Every week, people from the Loxichas were put in jail, disappeared, or killed. On July 10, 1997, we decided that we needed to install a *plantón*, a peaceful sit-in in front of the Governor's Palace in Oaxaca City, to demand attention to the injustices plaguing our region. Forty people had been assassinated, 150 arrested, and seven disappeared. The women, many of whose spouses had been assassinated or disappeared, set up camp and stayed there for the next four years. That was when women first took the initiative to be on the frontline, despite the fact that many had five or six children and had to leave all their responsibilities at home. We also sent commissions to Mexico City to speak with government officials.

In 1999, twenty-five of us relocated to Mexico City when the government transferred prisoners to Almoloya de Juarez. By 2000, we had seen some results brought about by our ongoing demonstrations; we were able to free nearly all of our political prisoners due to lack of evidence. The release of the political prisoners was the result of the *plantón* and everything we were doing to create awareness and to denounce what was happening. We are still fighting to this day but each of us has to work because there is no money for food and because we have to take care of our children and send them to school. Also, many of our husbands have migrated to the U.S. for fear of being victims of the ongoing repression.

Our growing movement in Oaxaca is composed of Loxicha women in support of the prisoners, the disappeared, and the assassinated people from our region. We are dedicated to denouncing human rights violations committed against the indigenous communities of the Loxicha region and to preserving our local customs and traditions that the government has tried to strip away. With the violent repression unleashed by the federal and state government against the APPO and the teachers' union, society is becoming more aware of the necessity to unite so that we can end discrimination and provide a better quality of life for indigenous people and all the people of Oaxaca.

Tonia

In the legendary March of Pots and Pans, on August 1, 2006,
thousands of women occupied the state television station, which had
long been used as a propaganda channel to maintain a corrupt state
government. Tonia, along with thousands of other women, seized
the station and broadcast from it for three weeks, at last making
the station what it had always claimed to be: The Channel of the
Oaxacan People.

At first I didn't sympathize with the striking teachers. On the
contrary, I was annoyed with the sit-in in the center and felt like
the teachers just repeated the same thing every year. But everything changed after the brutal repression that the government
unleashed against them. It made me put myself in their shoes. I
thought about the suffering it caused them– the woman who had
a miscarriage, the children who were beaten or fainted because
of the gases. If they do this to a union that big and organized,
what can you expect to face if you're a single citizen or housewife
making some demand or expressing your discontent?

For a lot of people, the violence of June 14th was the straw
that broke the camel's back. The situation in Oaxaca is unbearable. Rural communities live in extreme poverty. People from
my home village spend days making a *petate*, a straw mat that
they sell for 30 pesos. They can't afford a diet that provides
sufficient nourishment.

Yet Oaxaca is rich, full of natural resources. If it wasn't
for all the money the governors are stealing, we'd be better off
than the countries in the North. Ninety-two million pesos have
vanished without explanation—how much would that make per
citizen? The poverty and repression we face is the same poverty
and repression our grandparents and great-grandparents faced,
and it will not end unless we put an end to it. So I was thinking

of my own children and our future when I decided to participate in the third mega-march.

The third mega-march happened a few days after the repression of June 14th. The rain turned the streets into rivers. I walked beside my husband and many of our neighbors, impressed to see so many people there despite the rain. People who had never come out of their houses to protest before were now starting to participate. People were joking that Ulises had made a pact with the devil. Someone said that he had a pact with Tlaloc, the rain god, to stop us from continuing on with the marches. But there we all were, walking in the rivers from the Viguera Crossroads towards the *zócalo*, filled with excitement. And since then, I haven't missed one single march.

What really impressed me was when they started to announce the March of Pots and Pans of August 1st. "How is this possible?" I asked myself. I come from a village, and in a village, a woman is worth nothing. In a village a man drinks milk, a woman doesn't. She doesn't have that right. The man washes himself with soap. The woman doesn't, because she is a woman. The man has his towel to dry himself. The woman uses whatever she can. That's the environment I grew up in, where I experienced discrimination from my own parents, from my own mother even though she herself is a woman. My mother had grown up with this idea, and so we grew up without ever having our voices heard—*ni voz ni voto*. But as I grew up, I started to see that things are very different, that a woman can study too. I studied, I found a profession–a woman can do it! And she has every right to. She's worth as much as a man. And sometimes, I feel, women are so much more intelligent.

***

The August 1st march was organized by a group of women who were participating in a sit-in at the Finance Department. They had noticed that at the marches, many women, like me, didn't have a place to go, a group we belonged to. I would go and march with whomever, with the teachers or some organization, because even with all the organizations and unions forming part of the APPO, there wasn't a specific place for all of us housewives. So they decided to organize a women's march, and that was the moment that opened up a space for women in the movement, which for me was a welcome change.

So when I heard on *Radio Universidad* that they were inviting women to a march, telling them to bring pots and pans and whatever they could use to make noise, I was the first in line. I told myself, "I have to be there to see this rebellion, to live it." Soon the word spread among my friends. Some of them were enthusiastic to go, while others worried about what their husbands would say, and all of us were wondering how it would turn out, since such a rebellion of women had never been seen before. We didn't honestly expect that many women to show up. "We'll be two or three rebels and that's it," I thought. But when the famous day arrived, so many thousands of women joined the march.

When my friends and I got to the Fountain of the Seven Regions, where the march was to begin, it was filled with women—the young girls with their small frying pans and the old ladies with bigger ones. As the march started, the air filled with the sounds of women beating their pots and pans, with spoons that became flatter and flatter, and with the women's voices, crying out their anger at the government's brutality.

You couldn't see where the march ended or began. As we walked along, more women joined the demonstration. All kinds of women: poor indigenous women, middle class women, rich ladies, young students. Some of the girls looked to me to be no older than fifteen; some were even just five years old. There was a group of schoolgirls with endless creativity for inventing slogans. And I remember an old grandmother who carried an enormous pot. "What's that about?" I wondered. She looked like she was going to cook for everyone there. But instead she started banging the pot like a huge drum.

We got to the El Llano Park, which was filled with people watching and women waiting for the march to arrive. We got closer to the center, the slogans echoing on all the streets. Everyone was surprised, "What, the women, aren't they supposed to be quiet and submissive?" On Porfirio Diaz Street, someone threw a stone that hit me in the arm. I never saw where it came from, but probably from one of the many rich government supporters' houses on that street.

Finally we reached the *zócalo*, where the speeches began. It was there, seeing the power of all the women, that the idea of taking over Channel 9 occurred. It had been a secret dream of some people to take over the TV station that claims to be the "Channel of the Oaxacan People." In reality, it always works in favor of the government and against the people. Everyone was tired of the misinformation and the slander against the movement, but nobody had yet been willing to take the risk. But when one of the women shouted, "*Compañeras*, shall we take over Channel 9?" the response of the women was "Yes, yes, yes!"

Immediately, some of the women began stopping buses on the streets nearby and telling the drivers, "Take us to Channel 9!" Not "Could you take me?" or "please"—just "Take us to Channel 9!" You can imagine the feeling, going from never having your voice heard in society to "*todo el poder al pueblo*," all the power to the people.

I was with a girl who helps me with the house, and I told her, "Let's go to Channel 9!" But since I work as a massage therapist, I had an appointment that same afternoon, so I told Marcy to go home and prepare everything while I went ahead to Channel 9. We just had to be there, so that later, when it would already be history, we would be able to tell the tale. Marcy went home and after a while she called me and told me that the clients had canceled their appointment because the hotels wouldn't let the tourists out anymore, what with all the noise the women were making and Channel 9 taken over. I was happy to hear they had canceled so I could stay at Channel 9 and have fun.

When we got to the Channel 9 offices, the security guard didn't want to let us in, although in the end it was he himself who opened the door. The women in the front were asking permission for an hour or two to broadcast, but the employees of Channel 9 said it was impossible. Maybe if they would have given us that one hour and cooperated, then it wouldn't have gone any further. But with them seeing the number of women present, and still saying no, we decided, "Okay then, we'll take over the whole station."

With so many women, there was nothing the employees could do. They got scared and started leaving the building, hiding in their cars outside. The director of the channel, who you might imagine should be present to face the marchers, fled like a rat and left her employees there. Of course it was a scary situation for them, but there were no aggressions towards them. They were treated with respect the whole time.

Everyone was taken by the spontaneity of it all. Since no one had foreseen what would happen and no one was trained in advance, everything was born in the spur of the moment. The women organized into different groups. One group tried to get the radio to work, another, the television. I stayed downstairs with some other women. We were tired and didn't know exactly what was going on, but at the same time we were thrilled by the excitement. A group of women was going back and forth to the antennas by the river with one of the engineers. Someone was saying that upstairs they wanted to force the men who worked at Channel 9 to make the technical equipment work. In the end they had to help.

People from outside started bringing food: tamales, atole, mole, chicken soup. It was beautiful to see the immediate response and support of the people. The entrance of the television station looked like a supermarket, with an infinity of boxes of cookies and bags with hundreds of loaves of bread, huge packets of toilet paper, sugar, coffee, fruits and vegetables—as if we had moved in to stay there forever.

The afternoon went by. Everyone was calling their families to tell them to stay alert and wait for the antennas to start working. When it started getting dark, someone took the initiative to let the employees of the station out, so they wouldn't accuse us of kidnapping. Food and coffee were served to the line of employees waiting for their turn to get out. The security guard didn't even want to leave. He wanted to stay there with us!

When someone said that the channel was working, the phones began ringing, people calling to congratulate the women and their rebellion in all its splendor. I remember standing next to an old lady, whose husband called and said, "How dare you be there! I didn't know you were there! Don't you know how dangerous it is?" And the grandmother responding, "You told me yourself to go to the march, now you'll just have to take it.

And I'm going to stay here! All of the women are staying and so am I!"

We all stayed, and during the night, I spoke with my husband and asked him to bring me a sweater and a blanket, and another sweater for a *compañera*. There were a whole bunch of men supporting outside, bringing sweaters, blankets, everything.

A woman from the Guelaguetza neighborhood had taken her little daughter with her to the march, and now they were stuck inside. Everyone was telling her it was dangerous for the girl to be there, so the mother hid her behind some chairs. If the police came to evict us, they probably wouldn't do anything to harm the girl—we could only hope they wouldn't, in the name of God, because there was nothing else to do anymore.

That night, there was a big party at the TV station, with all the food and things they had brought us. Around midnight, singers came—young boys who serenaded the women. We were all standing outside singing, feeling enormous joy. At 2am two hundred teachers came from a statewide assembly, and everybody went out again to sing and shout slogans. Whether they want to call it a crime or not, we were already there, so why not just keep on singing? Nobody could sleep that night with all the excitement, and, at the same time, the uncertainty and the fear of the police coming to evict us. Finally we said, "If they are going to do something to harm us, they will have to do it to everyone."

I went daily to the TV station to stand guard and help out. The women were organized into different commissions: food, hygiene, production and security. One thing I liked is that there were no individual leaders. For each task, there was a group of several women in charge. We learned everything from the beginning. I remember somebody asking who could use a computer. Then many of the younger girls stepped forward, saying, "Me, me, I can!" In *Radio Universidad*, they announced that we needed people with technical skills, and more people came to help. In the beginning, they were filming headless people, you know. But the experience at Channel 9 showed us that where there's a will, there's a way. Things got done, and they got done well.

The people who were against the movement called us a group of resentful, angry women who were unsatisfied in our homes or in society. Bitter women. But we were happy, we couldn't have cared less. Being at Channel 9 made us feel good, empowered because the whole area belonged to women, to us. Everything was so great because we were making history. You could walk in to Channel 9, the Senate, or other occupied government buildings and nobody would say anything, because it all belonged to the people. Channel 9 started showing programs that criticized the government, and nobody was saying anything. During these months, our dream of power to the people became a reality.

In the short time that Channel 9 was running, until Governor Ulises commanded that the antennas be destroyed, we managed to spread a lot of information. Movies and documentaries were shown that you could never have imagined seeing on TV otherwise. Movies about different social movements, about the student massacre in Tlatelolco in Mexico City in 1968, the massacres in Aguas Blancas in Guerrero and Acteal in Chiapas, about guerrilla movements in Cuba and El Salvador. At this time, Channel 9 wasn't just the women's channel anymore. It was the channel of all the people. The ones participating made their own programs as well. There was a youth program and a program where people from the indigenous communities participated. There was a program of denouncements, where anyone could come and denounce how the government had treated them. A lot of people from the different neighborhoods and communities wanted to participate, there was hardly enough airtime for all of them.

The movement has had a huge impact on people, making them aware that everywhere, people are resisting. I think the women's movement changed the attitudes many people have so deeply ingrained. After the occupation, my father called me. After everything I had to endure as a girl and later as a woman, he was finally proud of me. He congratulated us, asking how we managed to take over Channel 9. That had made him realize how much women can achieve. Since then, he has started participating as well. Every time there is a march, he comes all the way from Juquila. I've had the support of my parents as well as my own husband and children. My husband doesn't have the same spirit of a fighter, but he's stood by my side during my participation. The children notice what's going on. This conflict affects them as well. We're in the car with my little son, who can't pronounce his R's yet, and he'll shout the slogans like "Uwises, you big, diwty wat!"

But many families are divided by this conflict. My sister and her husband are strongly against the movement. They don't understand what the barricades and rebellion are all about. She thinks people are only poor because they are lazy. I tell her it's a pointless discussion. She'll never convince me and I won't even try to convince her, best just to let everyone think what they want and respect each other. I haven't even visited her for more than half a year, because I got tired of her attacking me every time I go there.

***

Even after the equipment was destroyed, the women continued to occupy the television station, and we continued organizing. On the 31st of August, the COMO was formed as the women's organization within the APPO, and we have been active ever since. We've organized many big events, like a march from Oaxaca to Mexico City followed by a hunger strike. In the Mexico City subway, we were chanting the slogans of Oaxaca, and got a lot of positive response. For the traditional Three Kings Day celebrations, we had a children's festival where toys were given out—both to kids whose families belong to the PRI and to the children of the prisoners, dead and disappeared. Around International Women's Day, we organized a week of events.

My friend says I have *sueños guajiros*, that I dream big. For the COMO, my dream is to expand our organization to reach all the communities in Oaxaca. We could offer legal aid or medical care, and become a space for mutual support. Women from communities with some kind of problem could say, "Let's go to Oaxaca, the women from the COMO will be there."

YO TAMBIEN
ESCUCHO
RADIO PLANTÓN

Francisco

When the state television and radio station occupied by the women was destroyed by paramilitary forces in the middle of the night on August 21, 2006, the social movement showed its resilience by occupying all eleven commercial stations in the city by the following morning. Francisco, engineering student and radio technician, participated in the takeovers.

In July, when the *Radio Universidad* transmitter was destroyed, I was in my room playing games on the computer and listening to *Radio Cacerola* (Pots and Pans Radio). They announced that *Radio Universidad* was off the air and were asking that anyone who had 60 amp fuses to bring them to the University because they were having problems with the electrical installations.

At that time I wasn't involved in the movement, maybe because of a lack of vision or social consciousness, but I did sympathize because I thought as citizens we have a natural right to defend ourselves against injustice. We tend to live life passively. We think only of ourselves and we don't feel like we're part of anything bigger, like our communities or pueblos. Mass media only encourages individualism, and that's the cause of our social passivity.

I've worked with electronics since I was 12 years old. I work in an electronics workshop where I earn a living to pay for my studies at the Oaxacan Institute of Technology. My parents are working-class people who have made a lot of sacrifices to provide an education for me and all my brothers and sisters.

Radio Cacerola continued asking for the fuses and for technicians to go to *Radio Universidad*, so at 5:30am, I went down to the university campus to see what I could do. After passing through the check-point at the door of the radio station, I was allowed to go in. The atmosphere was tense in the room where the radio installations were. There were people guarding the installation. They asked me what I was there for. I identified myself and I told them that I wanted to provide technical support or do whatever I could to help, and that I had the 60 amp fuses they were looking for. They brought me back to the installations where there was a sharp, irritating smell in the air. There was yellow foam on the floor and on the equipment. A few weakly glimmering lights were the only signs of life from the radio transmitter.

The perpetrators of the crime were what we call *esquiroles*, people who are paid by the government to infiltrate the movement by pretending to support the movement while attempting to destabilize it from within. They had distracted the radio security by burning buses, which gave another person the chance to pour the corrosive acid onto the radio transmitter. The ones who burned the buses got away, but those responsible for destroying the radio were trapped inside and prevented from leaving. When we released them, we made two long lines of people that they had to walk through as they left the university. Once they were gone, technicians got to work inspecting and trying to repair the radio.

It was a long time before we were able to get *Radio Universidad* working again. Some of the parts were almost impossible to replace. We were working out a design for a metal piece we needed for the power source when the transmission from *Radio Cacerola* stopped—it had experienced technical failure from being on day and night without rest.

Those were moments of great anguish and desperation because it was the only informative media we had. We were disappointed in ourselves as technicians, too. We felt impotent and we wondered if only we had sacrificed a little more, stayed up later, working faster and with more urgency, then maybe we could have had the transmitter ready to replace the one that had failed.

The lack of communication was like a shadow that covered the city. The hitmen paid by the state took advantage of the situation by harassing *compañeros* that they found at the *plantón*, and it was only through cell phone calls or word of mouth that we found out about the acts of violence against some of the encampments at the sites of protest.

Radio Cacerola wasn't down for long, though. Due to the hard work of a group of technicians, we were able to start broadcasting again from what was now known as the "Channel of the Oaxacan People." It was with immense joy that we listened to the voices that we had missed so much during that difficult afternoon.

The other technicians and I continued with our task of repairing the radio, when around midnight, a *compañera* with a cell phone to her ear ran in to the room where we were working and said, "They're attacking like hell at the Fortín." We got up from our seats and left immediately.

There were a lot of people already preparing to go to the rescue of the *compas* who suffered the attack on the antennas on the Fortín Hill. We grabbed whatever was available: Molotov cocktails, sticks, machetes, fireworks, stones, and other improvised weapons. But what could we do with our "arms" against Ulises Ruiz's thugs, who carried AK-47s, high caliber pistols and so much hatred? Still, we had a lot of courage, the group of us, and in that moment the only important thing was getting to the place where our *compañeros* were under attack.

Everybody who wanted to go—girls and guys—hopped on a bus that had been taken for the use of the movement a while back. Meanwhile, people shot off fireworks to alert the neighbors who lived around the university campus of a possible attack. Then, along with some other technicians, I got on the bus that was being driven by a guy we call Red Beard. We covered our faces and left the campus from the exit door in the Institute of the Sciences of Education. It was closed when we got there, but another *compañero* called Soldier opened it with a machete. "¡*Vámonos*! Let's go!" we said. I felt a rush of adrenalin as we left for the site of the conflict.

We took the back roads through the Estrella neighborhood. We started going uphill, running the risk of falling off the cliff because the bus hardly fit on the narrow road. We made it thanks to our skilled but funny-looking driver, Red Beard, who wore round-framed carpenter goggles covering half of his face, a yellow fireman's helmet, and red beard. In truth, we all looked pretty funny in our protective gear: leather gloves and layered t-shirts. But what wasn't funny at all was the sound of bullets and screams that we heard on the other side of the hill as we continued onward.

When we got to the bridge on the hill, near the antennas, somebody shone their flashlights at us and asked us, "Who are you?" We all responded in unison, "¡la Universidad!"

We were told that the hitmen had approached the antennas, but the people standing guard thought that they might be *compañeros* coming as back-up; they never imagined that they would open fire. Our *compañeros* had yelled for them to identify themselves, but they were answered by a shower of bullets from high caliber weapons that seriously wounded several people and rendered the antennas useless.

They told us there might be an injured *compañero* nearby, so the twenty of us who had come from the University turned to go around the other side of the hill below the antennas. After half an hour looking for him, we came back up because we hadn't found anyone. We checked over the whole area with flashlights, but it turned out that the wounded had already been taken to the hospital. At the foot of the antenna, you could see tall flames. The Guelaguetza auditorium was on fire too. We decided to leave because there wasn't anything left to do. We had gotten there too late.

It was a lot more difficult to leave the area than it was to enter it, but Red Beard was able to manage it. When we got to the highway, we saw a caravan of buses filled with police on the road above us, accompanied by private cars without license plates. When we arrived at the *plantón*, we wanted to warn everyone there about the possibility of a police attack, but at the same time we didn't want to worry them.

Without a working radio, we lacked a means of communication and coordination. Some of our *compañeros* wanted us to stay in the *zócalo* to stand guard, but we were already on our way out. Soldier, Uncle, Satra, Cari and the rest of us all agreed to head towards *Radio La Ley*, which, we were told, had just been occupied by the movement.

It was the middle of the night when we reached *Radio La Ley*, but there were so many people in the streets and more and more continued to arrive from all the neighborhoods nearby: Jalatlaco, Xochimilco, Reforma, Volcanes, la Heladio, and many others.

Outside the station you could hear what they were broadcasting from a loudspeaker, "*Compañeros*, we need to take over the antennas! We must guarantee that our voices will not be interrupted!" Everyone knew there could be a police invasion at any minute. We parked the bus on the corner in front of the station, and all of us got off the bus armed with sticks, stones, and Molotov cocktails to defend the takeover of the radio.

Soon we realized that no one knew exactly where the antennas were located. Some said they were in Brenamiel, others in Volcanes. Some people said they were probably in the Rosario while others were sure they must be in Fortín. There were even people insisting that it was a satellite transmission. Those of us from *Radio Universidad* were deciding whether or not we should go looking for the antennas or to another radio station. In the end, we decided to take over another station.

We got on a bus and headed towards *Radio ORO*. When we got there, we knocked on the door of the station and announced with a megaphone, "This is a peaceful takeover. Open up. We are occupying this radio because they've taken away our last remaining means of free expression. This is a peaceful takeover. Open up!" The security guard opened the door and we entered, without anyone being hit, without insults- we just walked in. I even said, "Good morning" to the guard, though he didn't respond. We found out that there were three studios with three different frequencies. Those of us from *Radio Universidad* took over Magia 1080AM, the women from *Radio Cacerola* took over 1460AM and the kids from the anarchist-punk squat took over 98.5FM.

By morning, all eleven commercial radios in the city of Oaxaca had been occupied by the movement. The takeovers of the radios weren't planned. There's an incredible capacity to organize among my people. It was like spontaneous combustion. At first we didn't know what to do, but we soon became coordinated. All it took was a lot of minds working together towards a common goal.

Once things were up and running, we began to broadcast,

"Apologies to those of you who were expecting the morning program for children, the music to wake up to while you have breakfast and before you go to work. This radio has been occupied by the movement because yesterday our antennas were attacked."

There were voices calling out for freedom on all eleven frequencies in Oaxaca, voices that we miss so much now. Who doesn't remember the programs that *Radio La Ley* broadcasted? The Circus, The Urban Guerrilla, The Artificial Intelligence Service...shows that made us laugh with jokes and parodies about Ulises and his thugs and shows that made us think.

In the first few hours after we began to broadcast, there were an incredible number of phone calls, both for and against the movement. A teacher told me that a girl called in saying, "Lady, I've been listening to your point of view for four hours." The teacher responded, "Well, I've spent my entire life listening to the point of view of the rich."

At around noon that same day, we decided to give back the other stations that had been occupied because it would mean we would need more people on guard, and the two stations we kept would be sufficient to make ourselves heard.

After the takeover, I read an article that said that the intellectual and material authors of the takeovers of the radios weren't Oaxacan, that they came from somewhere else, and that they received very specialized support.

The article claimed that it would have been impossible for anyone without previous training to operate the radios in such a short amount of time because the equipment is too sophisticated for just anyone to use. They were wrong.

Oaxaca; 4 muer

■ Alerta máxima en la APPO; esperan hoy *op*
■ En el ataque contra barricadas arremeten

Bradley Roland Will, camarógrafo independiente de Indymedia, cayó
Oaxaca, abatido por dos balazos en el abdomen ■ **Francisco Olvera**

GUSTAVO

Gustavo, a native of the neighboring state of Guerrero, arrived in Oaxaca along with many photographers and independent journalists, inspired by the social movement and determined to document the people's resistance. Independent journalists, who provided coverage alternative to that of the commercial media monopoly, were specifically targeted by the government. In the most notorious case, American journalist Brad Will was murdered on October 27, 2006 at the barricade of Calicanto where Gustavo was also present, documenting the violence that the state unleashed that day.

I was working in Canada when I heard about what was happening in Oaxaca, and I knew it was time to go back home. A local independent radio station was covering the events: the brutal police repression of the annual teachers' sit-in had ignited a fire in the citizens of Oaxaca. After so many years of quietly bearing the injustices, people were rising up in response.

It wasn't only the police brutality that the people were reacting to. I started living in and photographing indigenous communities in 1997; it's clear that state-sponsored violence is much more than police attacks. There are so many people with no access to health care, so many homeless, and so many people without a chance to live in dignity. When you live among these communities, you start to realize the extent of the discontent and that sooner or later it's bound to explode.

I put together my photography equipment and made contact with a teacher from Guerrero. The teachers' union from Guerrero, along with those from Michoacán, Puebla and other states, was sending a caravan of teachers into Mexico City to greet the Oaxacan teachers who were about to arrive from a 530 kilometer march. I joined the delegation from Guerrero, and we arrived in Mexico City around October 10th, the same day as the marchers, with the idea of staying for three or four days to strengthen the presence of the marchers.

The *zócalo*, the enormous central plaza of Mexico City, was filled with people who came out to receive the marchers. There were thousands, kilometers of teachers marching, and they entered through the principal avenues of the city. At the head of the march, there were older teachers, as is the custom in indigenous communities. Many wore traditional indigenous dress and they walked in *guaraches*, simple sandals; most people didn't have special walking shoes. There were a lot of people with their feet bandaged. On either side of the marchers, there were people acting as security guards; sympathetic civil society had made a sort of human-chain to ensure that the marchers could safely enter the city. So many people were there: not a handful of rebels, but an entire society fed up with the corruption. Not just one state, but many states were present.

From center stage in the *zócalo*, the teachers restated their intention to do everything in their power to demand that the corrupt governor of Oaxaca resign. They urged for the unity of the Mexican people and thanked everyone for all their support. It was surprising to see the response of civil society. Even in the monstrosity that is Mexico City, it was really something majestic to see the incredible solidarity, and to have the opportunity to talk to people who know the meaning of social struggle, who've experienced firsthand the consequences of the interminable repression that our country experiences. You would think that in a place as big as Mexico City no one would have time to lend a hand. Maybe people sympathize to some extent, but who is going to actually alter their daily lives? So many people did, though. People showed their solidarity in so many ways. They camped out with the teachers, brought food, medicine, offered us their homes if we wanted to take showers.

From the *zócalo*, the teachers installed their *plantón* in the plaza in front of the Senate, where negotiations were taking place between the Secretary of the Interior and the leaders of the teachers' union. They put up tarps all over the plaza and in some of the surrounding alleyways and people from Mexico City brought food: bags of rice, bottles of water, all kinds of things. Men unloaded the food that kept arriving and women organized makeshift kitchens, separated chilies for salsas. Under another tent, doctors attended the injuries people had suffered on the march; they offered first aid and help for blisters. Everyone had their radios in hand, listening to the latest news of the negotiations.

It was a tense time because teachers were starting to doubt Enrique Rueda Pacheco, the leader of the union. I saw once when he walked through the encampment how he was chased by the people who criticized the way he was taking the negotiations. He never stopped as he walked quickly through the *plantón*, as if he were trying to escape. They yelled things like, "Traitor, don't sell out your people, don't sell out the teachers' union." The teachers who had been sleeping on the hard ground, who had walked for weeks for this cause, followed him shouting. Before any grassroots consultation, he announced that teachers would return to classes. They would be compensated for the days they had missed in the classroom and perhaps be granted something of their labor demands. But the teachers didn't want to go back to class until their broader social grievances were addressed; most importantly, they didn't want to give up until the governor had resigned.

For two nights I slept under a sky saturated with smog. Tiny raindrops spit down from above and there were no stars to be seen. From abroad, words and gestures of protest had formed a photograph in black and white in my mind, but after spending a few nights at the APPO encampment, I could see the shades of gray, the collective discontent that kindled the fire in our people. I headed south to Oaxaca in a bus full of teachers.

In the early 1900s, in a small town in Guerrero, my grandfather, a self-taught photographer, had the opportunity to photograph the national hero Emiliano Zapata as the revolution took hold in the southern part of Mexico. That photo would soon become the quintessential photo of the Mexican Revolution. Nearly a hundred years later, I was ready to photograph the social movement of the People's Assembly of Oaxaca, the APPO, or perhaps, the Mexican Revolution of the 21st century.

I had visited Oaxaca years before, when I was just becoming interested in photography.

I thought the city was beautiful then, with so many interesting places to visit and wonderful architecture. Everyone will tell you how lovely this city is. But today I recognize that the beauty comes with a high price—the price the Oaxacan people have had to pay for the pleasures of white tourism.

I spent the remainder of October in the streets. I wanted to photograph every moment in the life of the people shaken by this massive movement. I started spending the nights in the encampment in the *zócalo* in Oaxaca to understand, from up close, the demands of the people. They asked for the resignation of the assassin governor who had already taken the lives of several civilians. But just as it's always been in Mexico, the power is in the hands of a few, and justice is at the service of those who can buy it and nothing seems to change.

All month long you could feel the tension rising. On October 27th, the APPO announced that they were going to take more radical actions to increase the pressure on the federal government to force the resignation of the governor. They closed off the streets with barricades all day long, shut down banks, multinational chain stores and restaurants. I saw how they closed the banks. They would talk with the security guards outside and ask the employees to leave. They never actually had to enter the banks.

It was early that afternoon when I heard the announcement on the radio. They were asking for reinforcement at the barricade at Calicanto, where the neighbors at the barricades had just been shot at. The barricade was in Santa Lucía del Camino, a municipality that basically forms part of the city of Oaxaca. The neighborhood is known as a PRI stronghold, including a PRI-dominated municipal government, but it also has a fierce organized resistance. Traffic was a total chaos, of course, but, along with a lot of other young activists, I got on one of the buses that had been seized by the movement and headed over to the barricade.

We arrived to see a car lit up in flames. There must have been sixty people at the Calicanto barricade. Everyone was moving around, talking, organizing. I asked what was going on and the protestors told me, "We were here sitting around the barricade, when, from way down the street, a car drove up and these assholes got out and started firing at us."

Brad was there with camera in hand. In the midst of the panic, we shook hands and I asked him what he thought about the situation. It was my first time at this barricade, but Brad had spent time there. "Things don't look good," he told me. "*Cuídate*," I replied, "Take care of yourself."

Brad had been following what was happening in Oaxaca from abroad and wanted to come down to cover the people's movement. As media people, we saw each other around all over the place: at assemblies, barricades, the public funerals of activists, in the *zócalo*. We had chatted recently while I ate a hot dog at a corner stand, and he struck me as sincere and easy-going, and easily accepted by the people, which isn't always the case for journalists. He had traveled a lot in Latin America and had been involved in grassroots activism for a long time. In Oregon, Brad had lived in a tree in defense of forests that were going to be cut down, and he had defended parks and old buildings that belonged to communities in New York.

People in Santa Lucía already knew him. I remember when I arrived, the protestors shouted at all of us to turn off our cameras, but they let Brad keep filming. I took photos, but tried not to take pictures of any one's faces for their own security.

Everyone at the barricade was organizing to move towards the Santa Lucía municipal palace, where it was said that the hit men were hiding. Two streets lead to the municipal palace: Juarez and Siracusa, and the protestors tried to move down both. They set off firecrackers and carried rocks, sticks, and improvised weapons made from PVC pipes. I followed close behind with my camera. Men dressed in civilian clothing—but who were presumably municipal policeman—fired at us from down both streets. There must have been ten armed men who shot at us constantly.

Those images and the cries of the people—I can't get them out of my mind. The roar of firecrackers and the firearms, the bullets zipping past our heads.

Someone pointed at a rooftop where *priístas* were throwing rocks down at us. Protestors gathered in front of the house and tried to force the front door open. People screamed and firecrackers went off as they tried to beat down the door. We all prepared ourselves for a violent response from whoever was inside. I repositioned myself on the other side of the door to take pictures. Brad was there, too, filming. Finally, the protestor was able to get his foot inside the door and, with one last blow, force it open. The protestor moved to the side and you could hear two gunshots from inside the house, fired from behind the door that had been opened just milliseconds before. It was about 3:30pm on October 27, 2006. The afternoon sun began to set on the Oaxacan horizon; the shadows of the rebels in combat painted the walls along the street.

Holding on tight to my camera and crouching down, I crossed the street. There was so much uncertainty and fear; the adrenalin that rushed through us made our hair stand on end. They were firing at us from down the street, too, from next to the municipal palace. All of us—protestors, photographers and reporters—withdrew, taking refuge on Árboles, the street perpendicular to Juarez and Siracusa.

I heard the sound of a motor. A small cargo truck was driving down Árboles in reverse, followed by the majority of the protestors who were trying to protect themselves behind the tons of moving steel. The driver was brave; he reminded me of a kamikazi, the way he drove his truck down Juarez Street, risking his life, narrowly avoiding a shower of bullets coming at him from the men at the other end of the street. He threw the truck in reverse against the front of the house, and was able then to break through the door of the same house where we had just been. The driver got out fast, leaving the truck in the middle of the street for the protection of the protestors.

There must have been someone important in the municipal government inside that house, because at that moment, they started firing furiously at all of us. We ran, terrified, in all directions. We hid behind posts, trees and cars, whatever we could find amidst the crossfire.

On Siracusa Street, a similar front was being organized, which was also attacked with gunfire. Protestors responded with Molotov cocktails and firecrackers, but those weren't enough to repel the attack of the heavily armed plainclothes policemen at the service of the municipal president. The shooting lasted two hours; several people had been wounded already and we had hardly advanced towards the municipal palace.

The rest is a story that people in Mexico and throughout the world have heard from TV, newspapers, radio, the internet, or word of mouth. Those resisting on the frontline of combat lived it personally, and some of us saw it through the lens of a camera. Bearing witness to the brutal murder would change our lives.

I had sought protection on Árboles street and was moving back towards Juárez when I saw the protestors carrying a body. They cried out for help, "A doctor, an ambulance! Send for help! They shot the *güero*! They shot the *gringo*! They shot Brad! Someone do something!" Many people shouted his name, which shows how many people in the neighborhood already knew him.

His body was completely flaccid, so it wasn't easy to carry him. The people who were carrying him set him down on the ground and lots of people began to gather round. The only thing I could think about was that we needed to get him out of there as fast as possible. I supported his left leg and other people carried his other extremities. We moved forward, crossing Siracusa Street without even checking to see if they were shooting or not, then we laid him down in a safe place while we waited for help.

He had been shot in the stomach. It was a small wound; it hardly bled, but you could see the life draining from his face. I took off his bag so that he might be able to breathe better, but it was clear that he was about to die. His face was incredibly pale; he could hardly open his eyes and was just barely breathing. He couldn't respond to our questions.

I kept thinking how it must feel, knowing you're about to die far from your loved ones, far from your home. What can you do for someone who's feeling all that? I leaned close to him and spoke to him, "Brad, you're going to be okay. Brad we're here with you." It seemed like for a moment he wanted to regain strength; all around you could hear everyone shouting, "Hang in there, Brad! *¡Resiste!*"

Finally a car showed up and I held onto his head as we lifted him into the car. Everyone kept saying, "You'll be okay, Brad, don't worry." There wasn't room for all of us in the car. I thought about holding onto the back bumper of the car, but there wasn't any way of supporting myself and I knew they'd be going fast.

Later I found out that they had a lot of trouble getting to the hospital. First with the barricades, then they ran out of gasoline. A man with a pick-up truck offered to drive him then and an old woman wrapped him in her shawl. But a few blocks before they got to the Red Cross, Brad died in the arms of the people who brought him from Santa Lucía.

All those people who supported Brad in that moment were later wanted by the state, presented by the Attorney General as the ones guilty of the murder. There was a second bullet in his side that was shot later from close proximity, and they said it had been fired by the same gun. So the state prosecutor created a case to prevent the responsible from being imprisoned and to hold the protestors responsible. No one ever saw that second bullet. It's impossible to say how it happened, but I could imagine that the government arranged for it to be done inside the morgue. The state government is so dirty and so dishonest that nothing is beyond them. The state is constantly constructing its own stories; they could easily have arranged for the gun that had originally been fired to be brought to the morgue. The state government has infiltrators, too, of course. And they were clever enough to throw the policemen responsible in jail for a week. Then they were released for lack of evidence and can never be tried again for the same crime. And, unsurprisingly, the state waited six months before even opening an "investigation" of Brad's case. As always in Mexico, the government does everything in its power so that people will forget, or be too intimidated to press charges or organize.

Brad's death got the most attention, of course, but all over the city that same evening, the hitmen hired by the state government arrested, wounded, and murdered sympathizers of the People's Assembly of Oaxaca. Several protestors around the city were shot in the chest. The government had it all planned out--gunfire against the sticks and machetes of the barricades and encampments.

They knew exactly who they were aiming at. It would be impossible to believe that these were stray bullets. In Brad's case, they wanted to send a message to journalists who were giving in-depth coverage of the social movement, who were representing the voice of the people.

It's so important for the people who are organizing to be aware of what's happening in other places. It gives us strength to know that our demands are the same ones people are fighting for all over the world and to learn how different movements are built. Exchanging information and images strengthens solidarity and makes us recognize our common struggle. If we remain silent, the abuses will continue and deepen. It inspires us to know that people are rising up all over the world.

They didn't kill a journalist from the mainstream news. The commercial media, Televisa and TV Azteca, always present the government's perspective. They swoop in when there are murders to get their story then take their reporters away. Independent journalists like Brad clearly didn't come in with that intention. On the contrary, they came to get to know the people, to cover the conflict from up close. It's not easy to gain people's trust in order to document the resistance that way, but Brad was able to.

It's hard to say what will happen in Oaxaca. The government keeps pushing the people away from peaceful protest towards violence. Our society is tired, wounded, and the state is pushing us to take up arms. Everyone knows that that would be terrible, that violence only leads to more violence. But what alternatives are left given the context?

For a split second, I could see my own face in Brad's that day. We all knew it could have been any of us. It's hard to hold on to hope given the realities we face.

Hugo

On October 28, 2006, thousands of federal police forces were sent to Oaxaca to tear down the barricades and occupy the city. Hugo, an internationally recognized visual artist and citizen of Oaxaca, participated in the artistic resistance and civil disobedience that arose spontaneously all over the city.

I went to the *zócalo* on the night of October 27th. Everyone was saying the federal police would arrive at any moment. The air was thick with tension in the center of the city and at all the barricades. It looked like people were preparing for war.

There were so many people there, especially women. Housewives were gathered praying. A woman's voice over the radio urged the federal police to stay out of Oaxaca, spelling out for them who they were being sent to fight: poor people struggling just to get by, just to have enough to eat. They didn't deserve this sort of retaliation.

No one knew what was going to happen. We spent a long, anguished night there in the city center, awaiting the arrival of the troops.

When the police troops finally came the next day, October 28th, they had to enter through the barricade at Brenamiel, which was one of the most organized barricades in the city and also one of the most strategic because it was at the entrance point to Oaxaca from Mexico City.

At the Brenamiel barricade, there were women waiting with flowers to greet the federal police. *Radio Universidad* urged the people of Oaxaca not to enter into confrontations with the police, but instead to offer them indication of the peaceful nature of the movement. But, of course, we didn't want the police to misinterpret flowers as a sign of welcome, so we started dreaming up other forms of peaceful protest and civil disobedience.

I brought out a can of paint and hundreds of people started painting their hands white. We were responding to the constant propaganda of the State Attorney General, Lisbeth Caña Cadeza, that this was nothing but a movement of urban guerillas. So right there in front of where the police troops gathered we held up our painted hands as a way of saying, "look, here are our arms, here are the guerrillas."

A close friend of mine had been killed at one of the barricades during an earlier confrontation with the police. Before I was able to make a living as a sculptor, he and I worked together painting advertising—beer or soda logos on the walls of small businesses, things like that. I drew the logos and he painted them in, and we traveled as a team all over the state of Oaxaca for years. His death made such an impact on me.

It made me want to make a stronger statement. I came up with the idea of taking my own blood to paint with. Nurses from the state hospital were providing first aid at the *plantón* encampments and at the barricades. One of them helped me to draw blood for the painting. We were painting on the ground with our blood when the tanks started to roll in.

I wanted to show the federal police troops that were on the verge of invading our city, "If you want our blood, here it is, you can have it." I painted the faces of the people of Oaxaca and the words, *Ni una Gota más de Sangre*—Not another Drop of Blood, no more bloodshed.

It was a symbolic act. I knew it wouldn't change the course of events that were taking shape, but I felt in that moment that it would have been a crime to hang back, to remain silent about the violence unfolding. As a human being, an artist, as a friend of a fallen *compañero*, as a citizen of the city, I needed to make my voice heard and express my position.

***

It was a cruel and brutal confrontation. As the federal police troops entered the city with tanks and firearms against unarmed civilians, I imagine we felt something akin to what the indigenous people of Mexico and Oaxaca must have felt when the Spanish arrived. We didn't really know how their weapons worked. We had seen tanks before, but they had never been used against us.

That day, and in those initial moments, the confrontations were terrible. Right in front of the flowers, we began to throw rocks in a desperate attempt to stop the tanks. It was really incredible what those machines could do—lift up and clear away anything in their path. As the tanks begun to run over the barricades and anyone in the way, we quickly lost our sense of wonder and began to organize.

There were so many brave people, especially the women, who attempted to block the invasion with their own bodies. They put themselves in front of the tanks and some even hurled themselves to the ground. A few were almost carried away by the invading machines. On one of the bridges near Brenamiel, I saw a young man jump from atop a bus that was serving as a barricade and onto the tank that was spraying water and chemicals. He grabbed the hose and turned it on the driver before the tank jolted forward and knocked the man off. I will never forget the courage I saw that day among the people of Oaxaca.

I had been painting with my blood when the police began to advance, and in the commotion of running from the tanks and the shooting, a huge amount of blood spilled and splattered all over my arms and my shirt. Though I wasn't wounded, I was completely covered in blood and it looked horrific. I had

injured my foot in all the chaos and had a terrible time walking home. Of course, the blood all over my body made me look more hurt than I really was, and everyone was calling out to ask if I needed help.

I headed to the Institute of Technology where I had seen on television that a terrible confrontation was happening. By the time I arrived, they had killed a nurse from the Red Cross by shooting a teargas canister into his stomach. People were running for their lives; everything was in total chaos.

The city was in such disarray from the police invasion that I could hardly find my way home through the barricades all over the city. Finally, a woman showed me how to get through the barricades and back to my house where I could wash the blood off.

***

All over the city, people were resisting. The hills were alight with the reflection of mirrors. Someone on *Radio Universidad* had suggested that we might disorient the police helicopters that flew around city, menacingly low, if we held mirrors up as they passed. People also burned things with the idea of blocking the pilots' view. Of course, these were probably little more than romantic notions, but it shows the anguish and despair that people had, and how much they wanted to do something in the face of this repression. If there was nothing we could do to prevent the federal police from carrying out their orders, at least we could make our position of protest clear.

Throughout the intense moments of confrontation, you could always see so much tenderness present, so much kindness. At Brenamiel, for example, people from different neighborhoods:

Santa Rosa, San Jacinto, and Pueblo Nuevo came out every night with coffee and tamales to share. They organized into teams; there was a group responsible for bringing out materials for the barricade, another for bringing food, another for taking care of the garbage. Since my studio is out there, I had a chance to see the barricade on many nights before the entrance of the federal police. Even amidst the constant threats, there was a joyful atmosphere; someone was always playing music.

***

All day long on the 28th, the federal police invaded the city at strategic barricades. By the following day, they had made it into the city center, into the *zócalo*. They turned the *zócalo* into a military base. There were so many police there that it looked like a *plantón* of police. That is, the *plantón* of the teachers and the APPO had been replaced by a police *plantón*. For several months after that, they kept the *zócalo* surrounded by barbed wire with only a small space allowed for those who dared to enter and exit. Even the people who had applauded the entrance of the federal police were complaining. With the occupation of the city, a terrible psychological warfare was underway.

But people continued to resist. There is an image I will never forget. Even as the police advanced into the *zócalo*, there was a group of women wrapped in shawls kneeling in front of the main cathedral in the *zócalo*, holding their candles and rosaries, praying. Even in the darkness, people clutched on to hope.

The people, the teachers, everyone in the APPO moved the encampments of their *plantón* to the plaza and streets in front of Santo Domingo Cathedral, a few blocks down the road from the *zócalo*. Through a series of marches, we continued to demand that the police leave the city, despite the thousands of police that lined it.

I started bringing a first aid kit to all of the protests and marches. I filled the kit with bandages, cotton swabs, alcohol, as well as bottles of water, vinegar and Coca-Cola for the teargas. I tried to take care of as many injured *compañeros* as I could and carried the bodies of the seriously wounded to the nearest first aid stations.

At the marches that took place over the following month, there were infiltrators sent by the government to cause destruction and provoke the police. There were also people in the movement who fought back with the minimal weapons at their disposal: sticks, rocks, whatever. The sense of powerlessness, the frustration was overwhelming. People felt as if their homes had been invaded by the police forces and there was nothing that they could do about it.

***

"In the name of God, there will be no repression in Oaxaca!"

That's what Abascal, the Secretary of the Interior, said in front of the national congress a few weeks before they sent in the troops. Then an American journalist was killed and the federal government had to demonstrate that they were doing something, however ironic their response was, given that the journalist had been killed by people paid by the state government.

Officially, the federal government said they had to send in the police to remove the barricades. They expressed their intention to guarantee the "free transit of citizens" and as such, prioritized traffic disturbance as a graver offense than the horrendous slough of crimes carried out against the Oaxacan people by the state. So many people had been killed or disappeared; the state government seemed to have a carte blanche to do whatever it wanted.

The federal government's intention, they said, was to restore the "rule of law" in Oaxaca. But we know now, if we didn't know before, that the "rule of law" is nothing more than a tool used by the powerful to achieve their own ends. In fact, I would say that in Mexico we have the "law of the rulers" rather than a "rule of law" because of the way that the state manipulates the law and uses it against the people. In Oaxaca, the state governments have always used the law to advance their own power and privilege at the expense of the rights of the people.

***

When the federal police invaded Oaxaca, the people were already completely alienated from the government and highly aware of the extent to which their government had abandoned its responsibility to them. Even people who had nothing to do with the teachers, the APPO, the police or the government were affected by the political situation. The women in the market, the children whose classes had been cancelled—everyone became part of the polarization between the people and the government.

So people are painfully aware of the situation we're confronting. But there are a lot of people who don't want anything to do with political parties. Unfortunately, this benefits the ruling parties because the majority of people don't vote. Only about eight to ten percent vote PRI, but that's enough because no more than 30% of the population bother to go out to the polls. It's been enough to ensure eighty years straight of single-party rule under the PRI.

But there are more and more conscious people who raise their voices, who vote, who take to the streets. I believe things will have to get better, that something has to change.

Before the rebellion in Oaxaca, I had been somewhat distant from the teachers' movement and their yearly protests. I considered sit-ins, roadblocks, all of that to be obsolete. I thought that nowadays there must be new, better forms of protest to go about demanding real change in Oaxaca. But the attack on the teachers and the continued repression against the rest of Oaxacan society showed us that something had to be done.

I went on the radio to address my fellow artists. I encouraged artists to take a stand. "This is not the time for apathy," I told them, "No matter what your position is, demonstrate it. As artists you should shed light on what is happening."

There is a beautiful word, radical, to change things at the root. That is what we have tried to do in this movement, and our hope lies in that idea.

EL INOCENTE   EL CINICO

EL REPRESOR   EL RUIN

YESCKA

For months, Oaxaca was covered in spray paint. Graffiti artists like Yescka claimed every wall in the city to protest the brutality of the state and give voice and color to the visions of the movement for new forms of organizing and real democracy.

I am a 22 year old art student. Most people know me as Yescka. It's still difficult to give my full name because of the repression that continues in my state—or my *pueblo,* as we say around here. In spite of all the repression, I think that everyone who has participated in the Oaxacan social movement is the protagonist of his own story, and this is mine.

I've been painting graffiti and making stencils for many years. It's always been important to me to express myself freely, to make images that leave a mark, that tell a story of a time, an era, or a moment that will never be erased because they live on in our memories.

A lot of young people I know, myself included, had always been painting in the streets, but often without any real purpose. What I can thank this movement for is that it made us conscious, gave us reason and meaning—it opened our eyes.

Like many people in Oaxaca, I have relatives in the teachers' union, so I was in touch with the teachers at the *plantón* in the center from the beginning. Since I paint, my family members would often ask me to help them make banners for their marches.

On June 14th, a relative called us at about 5 o'clock in the morning. My mother woke me up and anxiously told me, "The teachers have just been forced out of the center. They're saying that there is a lot of teargas everywhere and they can't find your uncle."

I wanted to go to help, but my mother was scared and

183

wouldn't let me. I was frustrated that I couldn't go out. I switched on my radio to hear more about what was happening, but all the stations said very little, and the TV even less. There was music on the radio and all the normal programs on TV, as if nothing was happening, even though right here in Oaxaca people were wounded and brutally beaten. The center of town, the *zócalo*, was a mess, and entirely empty now. But the government never imagined how the people would react.

The next morning, there was a march and the people were able to take over the *zócalo* again. From that day on, many people started to show their solidarity with the teachers by bringing food and water.

After a few days, many organizations united and formed the APPO, which demanded the resignation of the governor. It was then that the famous mega-marches were born, with hundreds of thousands of people participating. For the marches, we started making paintings that showed our resistance to the oppressive system and small, symbolic stencils that criticized our terrible government.

It was incredible to see so many people smiling and showing us their support, giving us cans of spray paint and handing us their signs so we could paint stencils on them. When we got to the *zócalo*, people gave us more paint to use for murals and to write messages of solidarity.

During the mega-marches that followed, we got to know more and more artists. We started collaborating and making plans for ways to use our art in meaningful ways. I started to do more graphics and stencil prints that the APPO used for flyers and posters announcing upcoming marches.

I connected with other young artists and our ideas started to flow. I got to know Mario, a talented young painter and a member of the Frente Popular Revolucionario. He was a key figure in bringing together young art students and street artists. In spite of some differences in ideology, we were able to successfully work together on many projects. One of our first artistic collaborations was for the Day of the Dead festivities; we decided that in spite of all the problems in Oaxaca, we wanted to decorate the city and bring it some joy.

Day of the Dead is a very Mexican tradition that has been celebrated for hundreds of years, long before the arrival of the Spanish conquerors. Our ancestors created altars that they filled with offerings of fruit, food, symbolic objects, tobacco, *mezcal*, all kinds of things to honor their dead. The first day of the festival is for the spirits of children who have died, who are believed to visit our world on the first of November. On the second, the spirits of the adults come back to earth to take in the aromas, the light, the essence of everything left to them in those altars.

It was during the meetings and preparations for Day of the Dead that, as artists, we started working together in a more united and organized way. We called ourselves ASARO, the Assembly of Revolutionary Artists of Oaxaca. We shared the idea that assemblies are a good way to connect and organize.

The movement produced so many mixed feelings: tragedy with joy, laughter with tears, order with chaos. The capacity for creativity was enormous and the arts were flourishing. We thought about freedom. We broke away from traditional rules and impositions and we found out about the liberating power of art. We experimented with new materials and forms of art, creating images to raise consciousness. Song, dance, and theater were created for the people and by the people. In a way I feel like we revolutionized art and recovered its true meaning. We were finished with self-serving, commercial art. That was when

I began to understand what I now believe is truly the meaning of art: making people more sensitive, raising consciousness, and creating new spaces for artistic expression.

Those were difficult times. People were running out of food, and, more importantly, they were running out of patience. An American journalist was even assassinated by the government. Somehow, his murder became another excuse for the federal police to invade our city, and Oaxaca's shades of gray grew dark before they turned to red...

By the time the Federal Police invaded, even the most tolerant people had lost their patience. I was one of them. My conscience and my feelings compelled me to help my people, so I went to the Technology Institute, which had already become a battlefield where the federal police fought against the people.

All of a sudden, I felt a teargas canister hit my chest. I thought my heart had stopped, that I was going to die—but why was there no blood? I touched my chest; my heart hurt and was beating quickly. I asked myself, "Why didn't the bullet kill me?" I had heard that, when fired at close range, teargas canisters can kill people. But I didn't die, it wasn't my time. I had been holding my radio on my chest to listen to *Radio Universidad*. When I looked down I saw it had been completely destroyed in my hand—my radio had saved my life. In that moment, it seemed like I had been given a second chance to keep fighting for my ideals—and I did.

This year on Day of the Dead, the traditional festivities took on new meaning. The intimidating presence of the federal police troops filled the air; an atmosphere of sadness and chaos hung over the city. But we managed to overcome our fear and our loss. People wanted to carry on with the traditions, not only for their ancestors, but also for all those fallen in the movement in recent months.

Although it sounds a bit contradictory, Day of the Dead is when there is the most life in Oaxaca. There are carnivals, and people dress up in different costumes, such as devils or skeletons full of colorful feathers. They parade through the streets dancing or creating theatrical performances of comical daily happenings—this year, with a socio-political twist.

We didn't let the federal police forces standing guard stop our celebrating or our mourning. The whole tourist pathway in the center of the city, Macedonio Alcalá, was full of life. Protest music was playing and people danced and watched the creation of our famous sand murals, called *tapetes*. We dedicated them to all the people killed in the movement. Anyone who wanted to could join in to add to the mosaics. The mixed colors expressed our mixed feelings of repression and freedom; joy, sadness; and hatred, and love. The artwork and the chants permeating the street created an unforgettable scene that ultimately transformed our sadness into joy.

It was a day that made an impression on all of us. It was really spectacular to see the celebrations of Day of the Dead on one side, and on the other, total repression and chaos. The police troops were right there in front of the people, witnessing what turned out to be an incredible festival in the midst of the police repression. Even they must have been entertained. I think they must have understood then that Oaxaca is full of artists and warriors.

All this took place on the first day of November. We had no way of knowing what would happen the next day, November 2nd, that another battle would take place. But that's another story.

SILVIA

*Radio Universidad, based on the campus of the state university,
Universidad Autónoma "Benito Juarez" de Oaxaca (UABJO), was
at the center of the battle for control over the media. The radio
was taken over by students immediately following the police attack
on teachers and simultaneous destruction of Radio Plantón. Radio
Universidad found itself the focal point of many attacks, including
direct attacks on antennas and transmitters and signal interference. Cinco Señores, the barricade that protected the university
and its radio, was among the most valiant barricades in the city.
Silvia, a sociology student at the UABJO began participating in the
Cinco Señores barricades as a researcher and later became actively
involved. She was among the thousands who triumphantly defended
Radio Universidad when it was under attack by several thousand
federal police on November 2, 2006.*

November 1st: Day of the Dead at the Barricades

On November 1st, my research took me to the barricade at
Cinco Señores. I'm a sociology student, and up until that point,
my role in the movement had been as a researcher. At first I just
wanted to show up and do my interviews, but I quickly realized
it wasn't going to be that easy. People were living in a state of
fear and intimidation. No one could be sure who was working
for the government, so of course people were suspicious when I
started coming around and asking questions.

Cinco Señores was located at the intersection of seven major
streets, and was one of the most important barricades in the city.
Since it also blocked the road to my neighborhood, I had to
walk a long way when things got intense or the buses couldn't
get through; I had even been a bit annoyed by the barricade. But
on November 1st, my impression changed completely.

I had begun to feel increasingly absorbed by the realities around me, and found that I was no longer able to see myself as an outside observer looking in on the problems. There was no theory that could explain to me what was going on in Oaxaca; instead, I felt that to gain a deeper understanding I would have to get involved.

I asked some guys who were gathered at the barricade if they had thought about putting up an altar for Day of the Dead. It seemed important to me to not only block the street, but also to make our traditions present at the barricade. Neighbors would be able to identify with the altar and participate. "That's not a bad idea," they told me. "Why don't you go over to the University and ask them to make an announcement on the radio?" So I walked over to the university campus, wondering what I would say and thinking that they might not even take me seriously. I asked the radio broadcasters to make an announcement that at the Cinco Señores barricade, we were requesting fruit, sugar cane, flowers, and anything people wanted to bring to create the altar.

I was impressed by the spontaneity of organization; I liked that anyone could just contribute ideas to the barricade. But I was even more impressed when I got back to the barricade and saw the people's response. It couldn't have taken me more than fifteen minutes to get back to Cinco Señores from the university, but by the time I arrived at the barricade, there were already people building the altar. People had an enormous capacity to organize, showing their support for the movement in any way they could.

There were about twenty of us constructing the altar— many of them were older women and housewives from the neighborhood. There were also students and a few other people who worked nearby. The barricade looked like a busy anthill, with everybody arranging fruits, flowers and candles brought for the altar, shouting, "No, no. That doesn't look good there. Try over here." We made an arch out of sugar cane. People came out with soda, cigarettes, nuts and *tamales* to place as offerings. A group of men, maybe bakers, brought a huge loaf of bread. I don't know where all that fruit came from or who brought out the wooden tables we used. Someone placed the Mexican flag at the altar. It was an enormous and beautiful altar made up of so many different things. It was unlike anything I had seen before.

We used the tradition of Day of the Dead altars to denounce the assassinations and demand justice for the seventeen people who had been assassinated in the movement up to that point. Someone said, "Listen, if this is an altar dedicated to the murdered *compañeros*, we should have their full names, their photos, and something that explains how they died." I was so touched by the experience that I agreed to put the information together. I looked in the newspaper for information about the people who had died in the battles with the federal police forces and before that. Around the altar we painted white silhouettes of the faces of each of these victims, and next to each image, we placed a card with their names and when and where they had died. We placed each of these figures on the ground around the altar, and people came with offerings of flowers as if they were their own family.

We finished building the altar at two in the afternoon, but I stayed until midnight. In the evening, there was a mass held at the altar where people could sing "Ave Maria" and "The Lord's Prayer". Many of the people who participated in the mass were not even religious, including me. But this day was about bringing together ideas, culture and tradition in an atmosphere of mutual respect. I can hardly describe how moved I was that day. Sometimes the images and memories I have still make me want to cry.

November 2nd: The Battle for Radio Universidad

The next morning, someone called me saying that the federal police troops were coming to attack the university. When we got to the Cinco Señores barricade, the police were already there. People came running to me, saying, "Look what they've done with our altar!" The altar was already destroyed. People were deeply hurt by the police taking away their space of self-expression and by the deep lack of respect they showed for our culture.

At first, there weren't many people there to defend the barricade. "Oh my, they're coming in and they're going to kill us," I thought, looking at all the policemen who were ready to enter the university campus and seemed to be waiting only for the order to attack. And then the tanks came.

The police started entering from the barricade at Soriana across the way. A lot of people ran over there to help, including me, while many others stayed at Cinco Señores. I saw the tanks entering, advancing, and spraying people with water and chemicals. Young boys were running around with shopping carts filled with rocks and the slingshots that they used to hurl rocks at the advancing tanks. We saw the police back away for a moment. I think they got scared when people wouldn't surrender, even though they had enough arms to kill all of us. It was as if we were saying, "If you're going to kill me, you'll have to take a few stones in the process." We knew we were fighting for something just and we were ready to give it our all. If we didn't know we had justice on our side, everyone probably would have run away.

The police troops advanced, taking over a big part of University Avenue, which is a part of the university campus. Those entire seven blocks looked like a war zone—there were helicopters flying just above our heads, and people were running everywhere. The tanks were advancing and clouds of gas came from police who were shooting firecrackers into the middle of the crowds. People were making Molotov cocktails and throwing them at the tanks to try to stop them. People were defending themselves with sticks and stones, and whatever else they could find. I even saw a group of people pull a lamppost out of the ground, and a woman who had brought her gas tank with her. There were also people who tried to speak kindly to the police, to remind them that they, too, are *pueblo*.

The injured people were taken to first aid stations set up inside the university. La Doctora Berta, one of the main radio broadcasters for *Radio Universidad*, attended to people and there was a team of medical students who felt it was their social responsibility to help in what you might call "times of war." I think if one of the injured policemen had asked for their help, they would have offered medical attention to him as well. Even so, the medical team couldn't avoid the quantities of teargas being launched by the police. The police even threw rocks at a car that was circling around the area to pick up wounded people.

The battle lasted for hours. I was filled with fear and courage at the same time. It gave me strength to know that people were not going to leave me, and that I knew that I wasn't going to leave anybody behind either. I think it was that thought that

gave everyone the strength to stay: the idea of supporting each other and fighting side by side as one to stop the police from taking over the radio and the university.

I didn't think I was capable of throwing a rock and still I did it. I never imagined myself in a situation like that, but when you see the opposite of what people want enforced by the police, who are working only to guard the interests of the rich and powerful, you say to yourself, "We are not going to let this happen. We are going to fight back."

Many of the students were present that day. The police were entering the university campus by force, violating the autonomy of the university, and the students were there to defend what was theirs. Many of us remember the police repression at the national university in Mexico City during the student strike in 2000, and people didn't want the same thing to happen at their university.

There was an incredible moment when the police were surrounded—on one side were all the students at the campus, and on the other side were the people who had gathered outside to support us. The police were trapped between the two crowds, so they shot six or seven firecrackers at the same time. An impressive fire was started, and the policemen ran through the fire, fleeing from the university campus. It was a great triumph for the people.

The police were ordered to enter the university campus because the government wanted to shut down *Radio Universidad*. Why? They were scared of the voices of the people who organized through the radio. This was what really disturbed them.

But we never surrendered. And on that very day, the radio was used to organize the people. La Doctora Berta and the other radio broadcasters were calling for the people to come and defend *Radio Universidad*. More and more people came from all over the city.

La Barricada at Cinco Señores

After that painful and glorious day, the barricades became a part of my daily life. I would go between all the three barricades around the university: Soriana, Cinco Señores and the *Radio Universidad* barricade. But I spent most of my time at Cinco Señores because it was the least protected, so that's where I felt most needed.

The barricade was part of a political strategy. It was a way of demonstrating the government's lack of capacity for governance through civil disobedience. It was a way of saying, "Well, Ulises Ruiz, if you are really governing like you say you are, why is there an enormous roadblock at the federal highway, built by people demanding your resignation?" It was a way to put pressure on the state and federal government, but also a means for our own protection. All over the city, barricades were built to protect the sit-ins, our plantones, and to prevent the police and paramilitary troops from driving around the city shooting at people under the blanket of total impunity.

Cinco Señores was an especially important barricade because it defended *Radio Universidad*, which the government was still trying to shut down by any means possible. And they kept constantly harassing and threatening the *compañeros* who were directly involved in the radio.

The whole area around the university campus was under intense pressure. I don't know how we could bear being there, with the constant threat of being violently displaced at any moment. After all, we were not playing around with just anybody—we're talking about the state government that has the all the police troops at its service.

The barricade had seven cars lying crossways to block the seven roads. They were public transport buses or vans, Coca-Cola or Bimbo trucks, and even bigger trucks. On one side of the huge intersection, all the trash and the empty glass bottles were gathered. Opposite that pile, all the things that people had donated were arranged. There were many people who couldn't be at the barricade full-time, but who came with donations instead. They brought toilet paper, soup, cans of food, cigarettes, medical supplies, whatever the people who spent the whole day at the barricade might need. There is a pharmacy right there, Farmacia Mega, that served as the kitchen of the barricade. And although it sounds funny, the trucks served as bedrooms.

At the university, the classrooms were used as dormitories, but in Cinco Señores, the trucks were our rooms, because we didn't have anything else. The barricade was in the middle of the big, blocked intersection, so the trucks were our only shelter, though they didn't offer that much protection against the paramilitary groups who came to shoot at us at all hours.

It took me some time to gain people's trust. With such a diverse people gathered to defend the space, many social differences became visible. There were people that could stop by in their cars and drop off some coffee, and others who may not even have had homes. Unlike many people, I've had the chance to go to university, and there were some people at the barricade who didn't understand why people coming from a higher social class would want to be involved. There was a young boy, Chino we called him, who was maybe sixteen and one of the street kids who stayed at the barricade all day long. "Why are you here?" he asked me one day. "You walk around so clean all the time, wearing those fancy bracelets." I told him I was there for the same reason as him, because I think Ulises has to go, and if we all help each other out, it's easier.

Not everyone was like that, but it was sometimes difficult to relate to people with Chino's attitude; they're stigmatized by the whole society, so it makes them suspicious of other people and a whole chain of prejudice is created. The barricade at Cinco Señores was about breaking that, saying that, in spite of all our differences, we are here for the same reason, to defend the voice of the people and to challenge the state government's idea of what "governing" means. People learned to get along, and being together all the time created a feeling of mutual support and solidarity.

There were challenges to organizing with such plurality and with such a big group of people. We organized ourselves into different commissions. For example, there was a cooking commission and an information commission. The information commission gave out leaflets around the neighborhood explaining why the barricades around the university campus were necessary. There was a security commission, which consisted of a group of boys around eighteen or nineteen years old and even teenage boys from around the neighborhood. They were there around the clock, and I deeply respect the work they did because the rest of us could get some sleep, knowing that the boys were standing guard. When a car tried to pass, their job was to set off a firecracker to warn others. It was dangerous to let a car pass, because you could never know if the people inside were provocateurs or had arms. That's why the barricades developed the system of alarm fireworks.

I was on the commission that took the injured people to the university campus first aid stations. Many times it was one of the boys from the security commission. They weren't prepared for any kind of confrontations, really. There's a big difference between those young boys and the state's trained public security forces. And the threats were constant; fear was always present. Phone calls into the radio told us, "There's a car without license plates driving toward the radio…" The paramilitary, trained and contracted by the government, or state police out of uniform, came by to shoot at the barricades in the morning and throughout the day and night, hoping that by intimidating us we would give up.

***

November 25th continues to haunt me. I saw a young boy shot in the leg, friends around me arrested right and left, bullets flying everywhere. The government needed someone to blame, and it came down heaviest on the people at the barricades, especially strategic barricades like Cinco Señores. They called us vandals and thieves and delinquents.

There was some tension between the provisional direction of the APPO and the barricades. Within the movement, there were people who felt like the barricades were too dangerous since federal police troops were everywhere, and there were also people who wanted to negotiate with the state government. We felt like, "What's there to negotiate? We want Ulises out, and that's non-negotiable, so how can we enter into negotiations with him?"

The government hasn't changed and the intimidation continues, but I think the Oaxacan people have changed. Chino, the boy who was giving me a hard time at the barricade when I first arrived, later apologized. On November 25th he was hurt and I helped him. "I owe you an apology," he said. "It's just that when you feel rejected by the whole society, it makes you do the same thing to other people. You reject people who are different from you." He told me he had learned many things in those months that had made him think differently. I also heard the punk kids read a letter out loud, saying that the people who used to discriminate against them because of how they looked are now fighting side by side with them. I think that these stories reflect, on a wider level, what has happened in Oaxacan society. This movement has made all of us see the people around us in a new way. Instead of thinking that problems belong to someone else, we have understood how we are all affected, both locally and globally. On the streets, we learned to be more human.

On July 16, 2007, several months after this interview took place, Silvia was assaulted, arrested and held for several weeks, along with 62 others attempting to occupy the Guelaguetza Auditorium for the second Guelaguetza Popular.

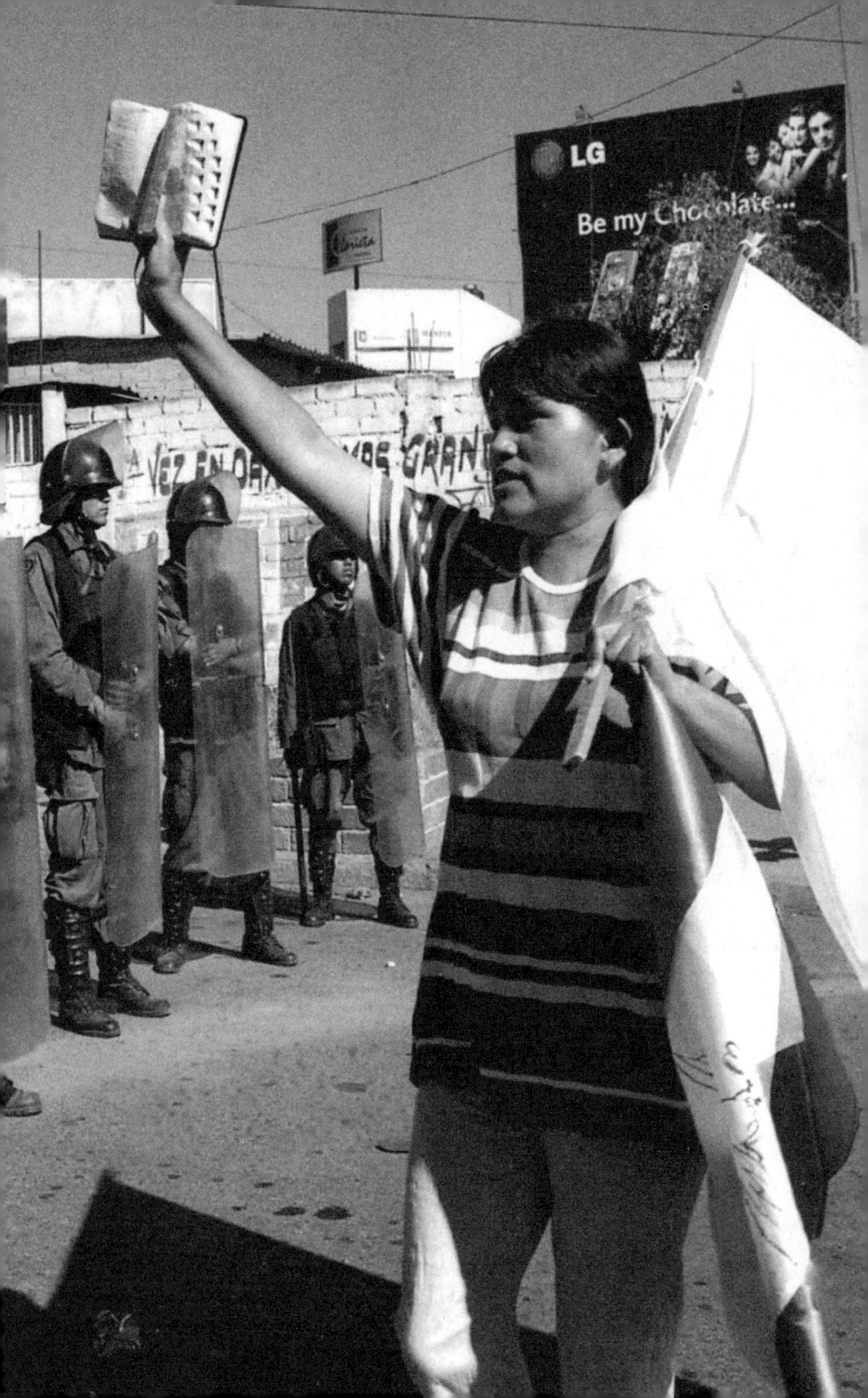
LG
Be my Chocolate...

PADRE ARIAS

Padre Manuel Arias Montes is a priest in the Oaxacan Diocese. As a progressive member of the Catholic Church, he has dedicated himself to working for social and economic justice for the indigenous and the poor in the state of Oaxaca. He has been an active supporter of the APPO and the people's movement despite the official position of the church, which has allied itself with the government and its armed repression of the people of Oaxaca.

I was born in a small town in the Mixteca region called Tlaxiaco. For ten years I worked with Oaxacan youth, helping them to develop their faith and sense of social responsibility, and later served a Triqui and Mixteco community in my region. I'm coordinator of the Presbyterian Council of the Catholic Church, which is significant because it's the only elected position, not named by the Bishop.

Within the Catholic Church there have been two well-known competing visions. The first views society and its relationship to its adherents through a hierarchical, top-down approach. The second positions itself as an ally of the disempowered, working with them to achieve social change from the bottom up. In the middle are those who are motivated by fear or self-interest, and serve as a cushion between these two poles. I have worked with total conviction to always take the side of the people from below: the simple and humble people, the indigenous people, who in the state of Oaxaca are the poorest of the poor.

My work within the church was the basis of my alliance with those demanding social justice during Oaxaca's political uprising in 2006. In October of that year, I named a commission to follow the conflict. In this commission, we voted to accompany the movement and take the side of the poor. This group of priests, of which I was the elected leader, pressured the Archbishop to form a special commission to follow the events of the Oaxacan uprising. However, there was dissension in the group based on competing visions of the role of the church in the social struggle. Ultimately, there was too much tension to continue as a church commission, so we who wanted to work on the side of the people separated ourselves and proceeded to work independently of the church. We dedicated ourselves to helping those who were suffering repression during the movement: those who were arrested and tortured, and the widows of those who were assassinated.

The history of our group of priests, who chose to side with the poor and indigenous, started many years ago. 1976 is a particularly significant date. This was the year that the Archdiocese of Oaxaca, Bartolomé Carrasco, began working to raise consciousness in the Church about the long history of repression, exploitation, humiliation, and deception of the indigenous communities by corrupt leaders who had effectively transformed themselves into *caciques* of the worst kind. These community leaders arbitrarily exerted their power over the poor with total impunity.

Oaxaca's culture is predominately indigenous with sixteen different ethnicities. Many of these cultures, in particular the Zapotec and Mixteco, were highly developed civilizations that suffered immeasurable harm from the Spanish invasion. Though Oaxaca still has an extraordinarily rich and diverse cultural and ethnic heritage, all these ethnic groups have endured years of oppression and exploitation.

Until 1976, the Church, like the state, had largely excluded the indigenous and the poor from political, economic, cultural, and social participation. Within the Church, there had been a spiritual conquest, which resulted in the marginalization of the indigenous people. Since the 1970s, however, the Church has become more conscious of this exclusion. The Church started to organize different groups of impoverished people to demand their rightful inclusion.

However, in 1988, Bishop Carrasco was replaced. We realized then that the institutional church would not permit any more Bishops who shared his vision. We decided to strengthen ourselves after seeing this internal repression and to learn from the people in our communities, the indigenous people. The indigenous tradition of community and equality-- a society which is dedicated to meeting the needs of each member rather than enriching itself-- is key to achieving the goal of social equality in Oaxaca. In indigenous tradition, a person's life is judged not by the wealth or achievements he has gained, but rather on how well he has served his community.

Our focus was not to teach a specific Christian gospel, but to empower the community to draw on Christian teachings along with their traditional indigenous spiritual beliefs, which emphasize social responsibility. We wanted to empower people to find solutions to their oppressive social situations through their own traditions as a means of recuperating the dignity of their *pueblos*.

A key point of our work with youth was encouraging them to link their beliefs with action. Another was to see God's vision in every human reality, and to see their responsibility to every human being and in every realm of life, including the economic, political, and social life of their *pueblos*. The indigenous value of community was crucial to this vision. As Freire said, no one liberates anyone else and no one liberates himself alone: the community must work together to achieve its liberation.

From this time forward, other organized groups from different parts of the state started to participate. This resulted in a more egalitarian distribution of power and perspective within the Church.

During the past few decades, the Church was active in forming leaders with consciousness and a strong sense of social responsibility. In this movement, many of our former students were acting upon the hopes for social change that they had gained through the Church. Many of the prominent leaders in today's social movement, both in Oaxaca and in the indigenous communities outside of Oaxaca, received their political formation in Catholic Youth Groups in the 1970s and 1980s. Examples include the leaders of the 25th of November Committee and those working for the Oaxacan Network of Human Rights and EDUCA, along with many of the teachers active in the movement. Numerous supporters of this movement and those active at the barricades are also members of the Catholic Church.

Since so many of the leaders who found themselves in the most danger as a result of their participation in the social movement had received their social justice education in our churches, it would have been a great betrayal for the Catholic Church to abandon them during this social struggle.

All of these leaders have a strong sense of the permanent injustice here in Oaxaca. Oaxaca has had such a long history of injustice including arrests of community leaders on fabricated charges, murders, and even massacres by the previous governor, all of which remain unresolved. With the government of Ulises Ruiz, which is considered by most to be illegitimately elected in the first place, the repression, corruption, and injustice has only increased. The government had acted with impunity for so many years; it was just a question of when things would explode. For a long time I have wondered: How long will the people of Oaxaca be able to stand this humiliation and oppression? How long will those engaged in the struggle for social justice continue to be imprisoned and assassinated? How long can this go on? And then came June 14th.

I think that in this context of so much repression, what happened on the 14th of June was expected. The repressive nature of Ruiz's government has dealt with the underlying problems in Oaxaca through threats, propaganda and repression, and the yearly teacher's protests were met with the same treatment. When the police attacked on June 14th, the Church was one of the first to publicly denounce what was happening and to call for the government to reflect on its actions.

On this same day, many civil organizations responded quickly, especially those that had Christian influences and roots in liberation theology, even if they were no longer officially affiliated with the Church. All pronounced themselves in solidarity with the teachers, and from this initial response emerged a broad, organized movement of thousands of participants.

At that point there were many of us in the Church who were offering simple support like bringing food, being present at takeovers of government buildings and radios, and accompanying the families of those who had been killed. Some of us participated in marches, so there was a sense of solidarity. The role of priests was to accompany the people, to give them support and confidence. But at the same time, there was another perspective in the Church. The Archbishop, and a small group of priests, began to align themselves with the powerful by supporting the federal government.

In our country, the word of the priest can have a significant impact, so we started to make pronouncements independent of the Archbishop. And that is how we began our communication with the press, some of which made an impact at the national level. For example, a headline in La Jornada announced that the Oaxacan priests had demanded the resignation of Ulises Ruiz from office. The number of priests who signed these public comuniqués was growing. We continued to firmly state our position that Ulises Ruiz should step down in order to create peace in Oaxaca, and we criticized the priests who had supported the arrival of the federal police troops, arguing that their entrance only aggravated the situation in Oaxaca. I think that this document that we signed provided a vision for the Oaxacan with a different vision of the Church—not a Church that sided with the powerful, but a Church that sided with the struggle of the people.

At the same time, there was increased persecution from both inside and outside the Church against those of us who had spoken out. Within the Church we weren't overtly silenced, but we were discouraged from publicly supporting the movement. The Church hierarchy attempted to thwart a document that all the priests had signed in support of the movement, and they tried to limit the amount of public support we were offering. We were also threatened by the government, which established a pirate radio station that acted as if it were the voice of the people. They called it "*Citizens' Radio*" when in fact it was meant to cause conflict by denouncing leading members of the APPO and threatening Catholic priests who were active in the movement. This situation culminated with shots being fired into a downtown parish.

This tension culminated during the night of terror on the 25th of November. This was a definitive night for the Church.

The churches in the center of Oaxaca—the most historic and central churches with the oldest parishes— failed to help those who were being jailed and beaten that night. The churches in the historic center closed their doors, despite an agreement we had made to offer help to those harmed by the violent repression of the federal police.

My church stayed open, but it was far away from where the violence was taking place. When a woman came to my church to see what we could do about what was happening in the center, I called the Bishop in the main church in the center and asked him what he could do to prevent the government repression that was taking place. Despite the palpable fear and terror of that night, he denied that anything important was happening. I told him that perhaps he was unable to see from all the teargas that must be in his eyes. Still he did nothing to help those suffering from the violent repression that day.

After November 25th, a group of priests held a mass to commemorate the struggles of the poor and those who had been arrested, wounded, and detained. One priest denounced the Bishop's shameful response to those who were under attack that night. To illustrate his point, he described how well-known artist and self-pronounced atheist, Francisco Toledo, had dedicated himself to helping the prisoners and the wounded that night, whereas the Bishop, a man of the Church, ignored the suffering of the people.

Toledo, who created the 25th of November Commission to demand the release of political prisoners arrested that night, has shown his dedication to the struggle of the powerless, and has been a leader to the many religious people that are part of this movement, while the Bishop has only closed his church's doors to the struggles of the poor.

Since this time, the role of the Church has been to accompany many of the arrested and tortured. We visit the families of political prisoners, and channel money donated to provide more substantial help to the victims and their families. Many of the widows and wives of prisoners are extremely poor and are barely surviving economically. We've helped some women establish small businesses and pay rent while their husbands are in jail. During this time we have also been able to listen and provide spiritual and psychological counsel to the victims and their families.

We also continue to provide support for those who have been released from jail. This can be a very difficult time for the released to reestablish their lives and find work. It can also be a difficult time for their families. At the same time, we are supporting the 25th of November Committee. We started organizing ecumenical days of reflection, despite the fact that these events were banned by the Bishop and that our first attempt was prevented by the federal police. But we did manage to hold one day of reflection weeks later. We continue working with NGOs and community groups in Oaxaca that are working to change the political structure that exists in the state. They are working for more governmental and financial transparency and legitimacy through dialogue with citizens, who, despite their poverty, have proven themselves to be a powerful participatory force.

There is a metaphor that describes the force of the indigenous people, articulated by the historian Antonio Gay. He says that an indigenous *pueblo* is like the stream that runs through the rocks, quietly gaining momentum as it advances. Sometimes the water has to run below the hills, but it always appears on the other side. Wherever it passes, the stream waters the seeds and fruits of the earth.

Likewise, though the Church hierarchy is an obstacle the people's struggle for social justice, there are priests who quietly bypass these hills to carry out our work on the other side. We continue to create our own history based on our own principles and values while the Bishop deceives himself by thinking that he governs our actions.

The 25th of November was the moment in which the Oaxacan people paid the price for their desire to construct a new Oaxaca. And the history of Oaxaca, if not of the entire country, resides in this new consciousness of dignity. Though the people of Oaxaca certainly were victims of repression by the powerful—Fox, Calderon, and Ruiz—the Oaxacan people also gained more force and energy for their struggle. I believe that November 25th marks the day in which Oaxaca became more powerful and brave, fortifying its spirit and its struggle.

CARMELINA

Carmelina, a Zapotec indigenous woman from the Central Valleys of Oaxaca, is among the founders of the Flor y Canto Center for Indigenous Rights. Founded in 1995 as a response to the prevalence of human rights violations in indigenous communities, Flor y Canto provides legal assistance and rights education in remote villages in Oaxaca. Flor y Canto has played an active role in the Oaxacan social movement by organizing assemblies among citizens to promote dialogue and the formation of concrete proposals for responsible government.

Flor y Canto was born of an indigenous process and is coordinated and directed by indigenous people. For the last eleven years, we've been providing legal assistance and education to improve the human rights situation in Oaxaca. We provide legal defense with the ultimate goal of changing the discriminatory practices and inhumane conditions that our people face every day.

Flor y Canto originated from a Catholic organization, the Pastoral Indigenous Dioceses of Oaxaca, directed by Bishop Don Bartolomé Carrasco Briset. He deserves mention because he played such a pivotal role in the history of our organization. In 1992, the year that marked the 500th anniversary of the arrival of the Catholic faith and white men to our land, Pastor Don Bartolomé proposed not a celebration, but a consultation with indigenous communities about their experiences with and feelings about Catholicism after 500 years of domination.

We began organizing meetings among the Mixtecos, Chatinos, Mixe, and Zapotecos of the Sierra Norte, of the Central Valleys, and of the Sierra Sur. We also invited the Zapotecos of the Isthmus of Tehuantepec. The Mixtecos of the Zona Alta and of the Zona Baja held similar meetings.

Then in 1992, we held the first Convention of Indigenous People. We outlined what had happened since the beginning of Catholic domination over the years, including the loss of many indigenous values, the destruction of our people's history, and the disappearance of many traditional codes of conduct. We discussed how many of our religious customs had been contaminated and mixed with the Catholic religion. For example, Christian churches have been built on top of our temples, and Catholic images have been painted over our own sacred images. Through these meetings and discussions, many people, especially young people, began to realize the extent to which our indigenous values and customs have been lost. Many of us didn't even know our own history since the history books teach that white men brought civilization to the ignorant "*indios*".

In 1994 we organized a second convention, in which we dealt with the political, social, cultural, and religious rights of the indigenous people. But on January 1, 1994, we awoke to the news of the Zapatista uprising in our neighboring state of Chiapas. The year that followed was one of heightened persecution of all indigenous movements, including our own. During our meetings we were harassed and spied on, so we were forced to work clandestinely.

During our 1994 meeting, we read the Mexican Constitution and saw that it guaranteed all people the right to education, health, and transit. Despite these constitutional guarantees, we had always used our own scarce resources to provide these services for our communities. While we were reading and studying the Constitution, we discovered another document called Convenio 169, which addressed the rights of indigenous and tribal people all over the world. The result of three days of meetings was to nominate a commission of seven people: six men and one woman (me), to pursue these rights.

Since indigenous communities in the state of Oaxaca generally lack knowledge about our basic human rights and how to defend ourselves against constant human rights violations, the group's mission was the promotion and defense of human rights through education and collaboration with other organizations and groups. At first we felt like we were throwing ourselves in a river without knowing how to swim; we were in charge of defending, promoting, and spreading our rights, but we didn't even know exactly what these rights were. In the end, we embraced the challenge. On January 13, 1996, with the help of many organizations, pastors, women, and missionaries, Flor y Canto was born.

***

What moved the city of Oaxaca on the 14th of June? The situation in Oaxaca is ultimately about the lack of autonomy in indigenous communities and the poor governance that has created these problems. People are angry. They are tired of asking for justice, tired of asking for respect for human rights, tired of corruption, tired of being tricked, and tired of being manipulated and denied their basic rights.

In some ways, June 14th shed light on the grievances felt especially deeply by the indigenous people. There has been no government response to the social demands and necessities of indigenous communities; it has done almost nothing to provide for the needs of our community. Our political autonomy has been systematically and continuously attacked by the state over the years.

Politics is no longer about the pursuit of a common good like it was in my grandparents' generation. Instead, *caciques*, corrupt local officials, control the different regions of the state. They have enriched themselves with the help of the government while the indigenous communities have suffered. Here justice is for the wealthy, those who can buy their rights from the government. There is no one who monitors our leaders. They go back and forth to the city, lobbying for projects like the construction of a beautiful municipal palace. But what good is this when social problems like drugs, alcohol, and prostitution are tearing our communities apart? Who is going to help our communities when our own leaders are only pursuing their own self-interest?

Conflict over land has been a cause of division and violence in our communities. The corruption of our local political process has created poverty in our communities. In turn, poverty among the *campesinos* has increased migration. First it was men, then women, and now even adolescents who leave their communities for the North. This migration has had serious consequences. Though migration brings much needed economic benefits, it has also brought an increasing loss of our traditional values. Migration leaves towns with a sense of abandonment. There are towns with only the elderly, women, and children who are left behind.

Our religious beliefs and customs have been undermined by different faiths that have been imposed on us by others. Faiths that, with all due respect, come from other nations and lands, and do not fit in indigenous communities. The Catholic Church has historically not respected the faiths and values of indigenous people.

Our sacred relationship with Mother Earth is being

attacked from many angles, and it, too, is deteriorating. The natural resources that could be used to benefit the indigenous people no longer belong to us. Even water is becoming more and more privatized. Government agencies administrate our natural resources, but they do not take care of them as they should.

Our language is one of the fundamental aspects of our existence, but how many years have we been attacked, criticized and punished for speaking our language? Some of us who still speak our native language learned it thanks to our grandmothers who did not speak Spanish. But in school our children are forced to speak Spanish and taught that it is more important to learn English than their mother tongue.

People are physically suffering. We have hospitals, but they are empty! You won't find medicine to cure diarrhea or other common diseases; the only thing you will find there are different methods of family planning, whose ultimate intention is to control women and their families.

Under state control, our communities have experienced only poverty, marginalization, and widespread human rights violations. It makes me very sad to see what is happening to my people; however, within these communities there are men and women who are fighting to preserve our customs and traditions.

***

Before the entrance of the PFP, Flor y Canto was working together with the Oaxacan Human Rights Network, documenting human rights violations during different moments of the social struggle. We attended the assembly of the APPO to listen to how they were working and organizing themselves, and we also did human rights observations at the different barricades.

It was terrible to witness the death squads, trucks of police in plainclothes attacking the civilians at the barricades, and to see the brute force of power and the human rights violations. In one community I visited, the teachers there had been beaten and tortured. The local authorities threatened us. When I wanted to intervene directly so that they would release prisoners being held illegally, I was threatened by local police wielding machetes.

As a human rights observer, I reported back on what was happening and I joined teachers and other *compañeros* to look for the disappeared, accompanying them to the barricades. We encouraged the youth to be careful and try not to provoke the authorities.

But in a social conflict so deep, what do the people hold onto? We held onto our sticks and stones, the tools of our communities. In the same way, the indigenous value of solidarity made it so that no one went hungry during the most difficult times of the conflict. I saw it all; my duty was to be at the barricades as a human rights observer between 10 o'clock in the morning until two or three the next morning. You could listen to the radio to hear what people needed, water, coffee, bread, or even a phone card. People would come with their carts, bicycles, or on foot bringing whatever was needed.

Participating actively in this movement has enriched my sight and my heart with the strength of the youth and the solidarity of so many people who came from neighborhoods and rural communities. I was especially moved during my observation of the barricades at night, where I saw people drinking coffee, sharing their bread and tortillas with *compañeros*. Their content but weary faces expressed a mix of so many emotions.

***

One of Flor y Canto's most significant achievements was the organization of the State Forum of Indigenous People of Oaxaca on November 28th and 29th of 2006. More than 400 people attended, including the former Bishop of San Cristóbal de las Casas, Don Samuel Ruiz, civil society organizations, APPO members, and representatives of the Zapoteco, Chinanteco, Mixteco, Chatinoi, Mazateco, Mixe, Huave, Cuicateco, Chontal, Zoque, Triqui, Amuzgo, Chocholteco and Tacuate communities.

We held a ceremony at the beginning and end of the Forum. The altar, in front of which each person who spoke at the forum stood, held corn and beans, symbols of nature that our lives depend on. The center of the altar was a snail, which symbolizes for us a path that never ends. The indigenous people know that this is a struggle that requires all of us to walk together, respecting diversity.

The forum was divided into four round tables that discussed autonomy and the organizational form of indigenous communities, land, territory and natural resources, indigenous culture, educational and communication initiatives, and human rights violations in indigenous communities.

The conclusion of these discussions was a formal critique of the state's systematic violence against indigenous identity, culture, and the political, social, and economic marginalization of indigenous communities. As an answer to this systematic aggression, the assembly proposed to consolidate community radios and demand them as an inalienable right and as a fundamental instrument in circulating information and news in communities that otherwise wouldn't have access to newspapers and internet. Through a handful of alternative media and with the work we're doing as organizations, we try to take back information to indigenous communities all over the state, but the state's monopoly on media makes our work difficult. The assembly also denounced state education in indigenous communities as a form of colonial conquest, and proposed autonomous education following the Zapatista example as a way to recover the traditions of the indigenous peoples.

We added these to the demands of the APPO to let the government know that the people were demanding accountability, to let them know that the eyes and ears of the indigenous community were open and that we were serious about our demands for change. The State Forum of Indigenous Communities of the State of Oaxaca launched the formal process of integration between the APPO and indigenous communities, and opened up new paths for dialogue and inclusion within the APPO.

***

The governor is using the poverty and misery of our communities for his own gain. But thanks to the ability of different organizations to work together and listen to one another, I think the government of Ulises Ruiz will fail in the end. This movement is made up of so many people with hands, shoulders, feet, hearts and eyes who are ultimately working for the liberation of our people, looking within ourselves to find how we can live with dignity and brotherhood.

Men, women, youth, and children keep shouting out their hopes, shouting that this power represented by Ulises Ruiz Ortiz doesn't represent us.

We have a governor who is imposing himself on the people, who wants to erase, to entirely wipe out a huge part of the reality of Oaxaca. But as a counterweight, we have a people who are beginning to cultivate new customs, new ways of life, and we are organizing to defend and promote our rights.

They have already cut our branches, cut our fruit, and they want to burn away our trunk, but there is a root that is very much alive, one that is in harmony with the cosmos, and that will be the root that will give us the strength we need to grow.

Many communities are creating local and regional people's assemblies. Maybe they're not putting up barricades or making improvised weapons, but they're creating another style of barricades. That is the work of the conscientious sectors of society, the APPO, citizens working for change.

There's a lot of work to be done outside the state too. People from all over are looking to the Oaxacan struggle for hope. They aspire to mobilize in their own regions for a better life with dignity for their own people. We've had a lot to share at conferences around the country. Many people have told me that all of Mexico looks to the south, Chiapas and Oaxaca, for the light that might show the way to a better country. Communities all over the country are creating people's assemblies in their regions. They're constructing other forms of resistance.

The neo-liberal project is a death sentence; it's destroying nature. But nature is wise and protests. And all of us are invited to share a new conception of plurality, of the interconnectedness of men and women, indigenous communities, the earth, the sun, the moon, the river, the clouds, the trees, the mountains, birds, and the sea. We can't sit back passively, we have to work with double the energy to articulate and retake the values that our ancestors have left to us. This is not a struggle in vain; it's a seed that's been sown and that will germinate and bear fruit.

PEDRO

Pedro Matías, long-time journalist and reporter for the newspaper with the largest distribution in Oaxaca, Noticias, has experienced, time and time again, the state government's efforts to control the media and violate freedom of expression and freedom of press. He has covered the entire Oaxacan social movement including the repression of November 25th, which he describes as the worst state-sponsored violence he has witnessed in his career as a journalist.

I've worked as a journalist for twenty years. Right now, I'm a reporter for *Noticias*, the main newspaper in the state of Oaxaca. I also write for *Progreso,* a magazine with national distribution and work for the independent station *Radio Jit.*

The harassment of the press currently happening in the state of Oaxaca under Ulises Ruiz Ortiz has its roots in the previous PRI administrations. I've received threats by three consecutive state governments: Carrasco, José Murat, and Ulises Ruiz.

I used to work at smaller newspapers that were harassed by the government and were eventually closed. Like *Contrapunto*, *Presente, Enlace* and *Expresión.* They were newspapers that were critical of the state, so the government closed them by blocking their publishing spaces and economically strangling them until they disappeared.

In the newspaper *Expresión*, it went beyond that. The owner of the newspaper, Humberto Lopez Lena, was arrested for publishing information that had been sent to him by the national newspaper *La Jornada*, in Mexico City. He didn't write it, he just printed it. That was in April 2004. But the governor at the time, José Murat, got together a search warrant and an arrest warrant all in one day. That was his idea of the "application of justice." That's what he did to eliminate enemies.

They kept Lopez Leña in jail. They accused him of slander and cancelled all of his bank accounts.

There were arrest warrants out for several of us. We had to seek legal protection and stay hidden, doing our work clandestinely.

That's about the time when the problems started between José Murat and *Noticias*. When Lopez Lena's newspaper closed, that's when I started working at the radio, which is where I was when *Noticias* offered me a job as a reporter. They offered me the job with the idea of strengthening the paper's critical analysis. I had always been a person who the government saw as critical, and at times they've tried to close off my job opportunities and prevent me from working.

Noticias had always had a certain prestige, being the newspaper with the highest sales in Oaxaca. But it wasn't openly critical of the government. On the contrary, *Noticias* had what you would call a preferential relationship with the state government because of certain publicity arrangements. *Noticias* benefited from extensive government advertising.

The owner's story goes like this. In 2004, José Murat tried to buy part of *Noticias*. When the owner refused to sell, the government increased aggression against all the media, especially *Noticias*.

In November, raids on the *Noticias* warehouses began. A number of things led up to those raids. There was an assassination. There were blockades in which pro-government agitators, the CROC, and even police participated. Officially, the CROC (the Revolutionary Confederation of Workers and Peasants) was the union that represented some *Noticias* workers. However, instead of supporting workers, it basically remained under control of the PRI and the state government. When it came time for contract renewals, the CROC only served the orders of Ulises Ruiz's government.

With the rupture with José Murat, *Noticias* finally became a newspaper that wasn't afraid to criticize the system.

José Murat turned over power to Ulises Ruiz Ortiz on December 1, 2005. Instead of pacifying the discontent or taking actions to return to normality with respect to the treatment of media, Ulises Ruiz Ortiz continued the attacks against the press and made the problem his own.

First, his administration tried to strangle the paper economically. Ulises Ruiz Ortiz had bet that in three months, the newspaper would die without the money received from state government publicity and private sector advertising. But it didn't happen like that. And that's when the persecution against *Noticias* really began.

The first march in protest of the administration of Ulises Ruiz was carried out by *Noticias*. We were protesting warehouse raids. That's where the paper and chemicals for printing are stored. The government figured that, since *Noticias* buys a six month's supply at a time, by destroying the materials or preventing access to them, we wouldn't be able to work. But we started buying our supplies from Puebla and other states, and the newspaper came out day after day without fail.

Later in 2005, when it came time for contract renewals, the government, through the CROC, created a huge fictitious strike to shut down *Noticias*. Under the orders of Ulises Ruiz, the CROC demanded dramatic wage increases in order to justify starting a strike. The *Noticias* workers didn't want to strike. That's why the CROC had to use truck drivers, deliverers, and workers from other sectors to seize the newspaper building.

In June, we heard a rumor that they were going to try to

shut down the *Noticias* building, so all of the workers decided to stay there all day writing and editing. It was 6 o'clock in the evening and they still hadn't arrived. We waited: 7pm, 8, 9, 10. By 11 at night we were hungry, so we formed two committees so that some of us could get something to eat and bring it back to everybody else. I went down the street with a colleague to buy tacos and *tlayudas* for all the people at the office.

We had just walked two blocks when suddenly a ton of plainclothes police arrived; marching and shouting, they took over the newspaper. I didn't know any of them, but some of our reporters who cover the police section were able to identify some of them as police. There wasn't a single person among them who had a work contract with *Noticias*.

We wanted to go back inside but they wouldn't let us in. Thirty-one of our colleagues were in the building. Our colleagues told us it was hell in there. The police were aggressive and assaulted them. There was obviously no way any of our colleagues could get any sleep; they had to be alert because they were terrorized all night. There were several people who had diabetes, who weren't allowed to leave even though they needed their injections.

The agitators held them all hostages: the journalists, technicians, directors, graphic designers, and people responsible for the printing. Police and pro-government agitators guarded the building. Our colleagues were forced to stay in the building for one month, after which they were released because of so much international pressure.

In spite of everything, there wasn't a single day that the newspaper didn't come out. Those of us who weren't being held hostage reported from outside. We had the paper printed in Tuxtepec.

The state and ministerial police tried to prevent the newspaper from circulating. We had copies driven in trucks or flown to the airport. Those of us with cars drove to the airport for two or three bundles and took them to Xoxo or another place where we were secretly operating from.

The newspaper had never done better. They tell me that *Noticias* sold, on average, 25,000 copies a day, but during that period, we sold as many as 80,000. The police were confiscating papers, but people looked for them at intersections or newspaper stands that sold them covertly. People would even buy papers that were several days old.

***

It's upsetting to think that the constitution is only for the libraries or for the use of the political class when it suits them and that it simply doesn't exist for the people. It says in the constitution that people have the right to express themselves, but in reality, if people speak up, they risk all kinds of persecution.

I find it surprising that the politicians expect us to respect the constitution of our country, its institutions, the results of the elections, and the political class, but we can't question anything without being accused of being rebels. For Mexicans, and especially for Oaxacans, our status as citizens only lasts for a day—the day we go out to vote. The next day, if we protest, if we try to express what it is we object to in the system, we are accused of being insurgents, guerrillas and criminals. Our institutions exist only to serve an elite political class.

The victimization of the poor has only gotten worse. There is more violence and repression than ever, and those who protest are attacked.

For the last year, I've been covering this movement, putting out information as it becomes available. I saw the attack on the teachers on June 14th—the violence of the state police and how they were forced to back down because they never imagined that the teachers would react the way they did, never imagined the solidarity of the people.

People's anger had been festering for a long time. As soon as Ulises Ruiz came to power human rights violations began to escalate, ones that have yet to be rectified, including assassinations in the Sierra Sur and in the Isthmus. He immediately started attacking the cultural symbols of the city: the *zócalo*, the Plaza de la Danza, the Fountain of the Seven Regions, and the Guelaguetza. There was an enormous tree in the *zócalo* that he had cut down. People were furious. You could say that tree was the first spark of what later turned into raging fires in the city of Oaxaca.

After June 14th, people felt like there was no alternative and they began to organize. They organized huge marches; the fourth mega-march had 800,000 people in the capital. Some say up to a million. But 800,000 people marching to remove one person from power is evidence that the political system is coming apart at the seams.

The 25th of November was a tragic day for the people. I've seen all kinds of clashes and confrontations, but I have never in my life had an experience like that day. November 25th made me feel powerless, afraid. You really don't know what to do in a situation like that.

There were people infiltrating the movement. The government had it all figured out. They had the idea that it would serve their interests if some of the government buildings were set on fire, that they would benefit from confrontations with the PFP. All that would give the government further pretext to repress the people's movement. No one is stupid enough to believe that a Molotov cocktail can burn down a building the size of the Supreme Court; a building, as it happens, that contains documents that the government would just as soon see disappear. Who burned down those buildings, then? It had to be government infiltrators. Is there any proof? Of course there's no proof! They're not going to turn themselves in. But, undeniably, it was useful for the government, because it allowed them to justify more violence against the people.

We were there the whole day on November 25th. The police attacked and attacked, pushing us back to the Pastoral Center. Then there were tanks and they started shooting at us. All of us had to run. You couldn't just stand there and say, "I'm with the press!" because they were arresting everybody. They beat up a colleague of mine from *El Financiero*. He had to get 10 stitches.

At 5 o'clock in the afternoon, a group of teenagers started looking for trouble. They wanted to confront the PFP, and that's when it all exploded. There was a big confrontation, with teargas, gunfire (yes, there was shooting) and after that there were fires. Between 5pm and 11pm, Oaxaca went up in flames. There was a cloud of teargas and another of thick black smoke.

They forced us back. The 15, 16, and 17 year-old boys with their make-shift shields were on the front-line, confronting the police. Then there was a second line of protesters firing improvised weapons and behind them were the women, who were throwing stones. They had taken hundreds of bricks from a construction site and stones from the road, and were breaking them into pieces.

The crowd of men and women were shouting and moving forward. Behind them, the older people were carrying water. They also had towels for people to cover their mouths. Behind them were the medical students from the university, who were attending to the people who were having terrible reactions to the teargas and who had head injuries. They gave us soft drinks and vinegar to alleviate the effects of the gas, and they offered to help us if we were hurt. When the police came, we had to retreat. The police burned the APPO encampment in Santo Domingo Plaza and forced us to retreat.

November 25th was a very important day in my life as a journalist. I saw a lot of things that day. I wanted to be part of the people, to stand with them. It's difficult to explain what it was like. In my twenty years as a reporter, I have never seen anything like it. The people took to the streets, demonstrated, and protested. There was no official organization, they just organized themselves. It was really amazing.

At the Social Security Building, two groups of police came towards us: one from Llano Park and the other from the Santo Domingo Plaza. So, about a hundred of us—men, women and even elderly people—had to flee down the road to Fortín Hill. It was around 9:30pm when we got there.

I joined a group of independent journalists from France, New York and Spain. There were eight or nine of us. I decided I would stay with them for protection, since I figured they were less likely to attack foreigners. But I knew they could arrest or even disappear me.

At the intersection where the Hotel Fortín is, about ten or twelve of us got into a red van and headed for the neighborhood called Estrella, but we couldn't make it very far, so we ended up walking to look for a taxi. Then the PFP and state police vans came from either Crespo Street or Tinoco y Palacios. They surrounded us. They beat me mercilessly. We didn't know what to do. We ran up to Fortin Hill. Everyone was shouting.

The international journalists were terrified by what they saw. A van pulled up and some people were knocked down onto the pavement. Women were calling out in desperation. We couldn't take any photos. Even the photographers who were there were afraid to take photos in case they were caught.

I didn't know what to do. We were totally powerless. We couldn't help or do anything at all. To avoid being shot or killed, we had to hide out at Fortin Hill, like criminals, so they wouldn't find us. In the distance, even as far away as the Pastoral Center, you could hear people crying out…it was so awful.

People were coming out of their houses and saying, "The police are here, go over that way." So we spent a half an hour trying to hide from the police. I think the international reporters had never seen anything like this in their lives. I worried about them later, because I didn't see them the next day. I think they must have left on the first flight out of Oaxaca.

I got a phone call from friends at *Radio Red* in Mexico City. "Pedro, how are things going, are you alright?" he asked me. "I'm OK, but I really can't talk," I said. I spoke to my boss at *Noticias* and told him I couldn't go anywhere, that I was trapped, that the police were beating and arresting everybody. They sent a motorcycle for me around 10:30 and I managed to get to the newspaper office.

When we had been up on the hill, we'd seen a lot of smoke in the air. It looked like the whole state was on fire. But the hardest thing for me was that they were accusing innocent people, even an old lady I saw, of starting the fires. They really went too far.

They government had a chance to resolve the situation, but they ended up imprisoning people who were only asking for justice. Meanwhile, Vicente Fox allows drug traffickers to go free. The politicians have never come down hard on drug traffickers. For this government, it's people who are asking for social change that constitute the real threat.

AURELIA

During the rioting of November 25th, hundreds of people were arrested and tortured, including many who had nothing to do with the social movement and who had not attended the march. Aurelia, who works as a maid in the city center, left the home where she was working to find herself in the midst of the terror that unfolded that afternoon.

On the 25th of November, I was working inside a house, so I didn't know what was happening outside. I work as a maid since I don't know how to read and write. I'm 50 years old and a widow. I have three children.

I had just left work when they arrested me, only half a block from the house where I work. I was walking down the street and saw people running all over the place. I didn't know why—I had been inside the house all day. Suddenly, I saw police everywhere. They carried rifles and started firing at everyone. I think it was some kind of gas they were shooting, I really don't know. I got trapped in the smoke. I felt myself asphyxiating and my eyes filled with tears. I couldn't move. I was so scared.

The police were everywhere with their huge rifles. All of them carried rifles. They arrested me and took me towards the *zócalo*. They grabbed me by the hair and yelled at me to walk. They were cursing, shouting all kinds of vulgarities at me. I begged them to let me go: "My family doesn't know where I am. I just got out of work. I have nothing to do with any of this!" But they just kicked me in response. In the *zócalo*, they tied me up. There were policewomen who grabbed me by the hair and threw me to the ground where they tied my hands and feet behind me, saying, "Come on, son of a…sing to your APPO." I cried, "I just got out of work, I don't know what you're talking to me about!"

I could see there were so many women they had forced to kneel down on the cobblestone. They put me up against the wall of the cathedral and made me kneel for two hours.

I was carrying a backpack and a sweater. They took my backpack, asking, "What do you have here, you stupid…" They started to search me. They said, "What do you have in your purse?" I answered that it was my week's wages. "That's money that your APPO gave to you," they replied. And they took all the money that I had earned that week.

They had me like that for two hours kneeling on the ground. It was so cold. I had a white sweatshirt, but they took it away from me. I could see that there were so many wounded men, covered in blood, groaning. The police passed by and kicked them. They grabbed their hair and threw them against the ground. I thought of my children. I thought, "My god, what if one of my children were here." It was about the time that they should have gotten off work. I wondered if one of my children or nephews or nieces was there.

They would pass by and yell at everyone, "Shut up you sons of bitches, I don't know what you're complaining about. This isn't supposed to be some party." The police shouted all kinds of vulgarities at us.

One of the police officers—who wasn't really a policeman because I could see that he wore jeans—he put his knee in my back. "Careful not to move," he told me. And I couldn't stand it anymore. I felt exhausted because they had me tied up and he kept crushing me with his knee. My back couldn't take it anymore. I begged them, "Just let me rest for a minute," but they responded, "We're not going to let you rest, you're not at your house, you bitch. Here you do whatever we tell you to do!"

After some hours, they got us all up and brought us, practically crawling, to a red truck in the *zócalo*. I didn't see what model it was, just that it was red. When I got to the truck I could see all the women they had thrown in, one on top of the other like animals, with their hands and feet tied. They pushed me on top of the others, and the ones on the bottom cried out, "Please, move over a little, I can't stand this anymore, my feet hurt. I can't feel my body anymore." It was awful to be on top of all of those women. We were like that for another hour at least...the time went by so slowly.

They started up the truck and began driving. I don't know where because we were thrown in there with our faces to the floor. "Don't move," they told us and one of the police officers put her foot over me to prevent me from moving. It seemed like forever and it was so cold. Everyone was moaning, the poor women on the bottom kept crying out, "Please help us, I can't feel my legs anymore, I can't feel my body." The police officers just responded, "You may as well die, you old hags. There's no problem if you die, there are plenty of garbage dumps on the way where we can throw you. It's dark and no one will see us. There are plenty of garbage cans—we can just toss you out."

Finally, we arrived at the place where they were taking us. Everything was dark. I couldn't see anything to tell where we were. After a long time you could hear the engine of a large vehicle. They took us off the truck, tied up like we were, pulling us by the hair and kicking and pushing us so that we would hurry up and get off. I could see a huge gate. I thought, "God knows where they're putting us..." I was scared. The other women cried too: "Where are my children?" They were all asking about their children. You could hear them saying, "Please just tell me where my children are. I have two children, one is eight years old and one is twelve." And, "I have a twelve year old daughter- where is she? Tell me where she is." The police officers responded, "Would you bitches just shut up and walk." And they pushed us in the gate and sat us up against the wall. They untied us a little and put our hands behind our heads.

There was a sort of wall that we could see over when they started to bring in the men on the other side. It was my terrible luck to see my son there, in front of me. I felt horrible because my son had just gotten off work, and I could see he had been beaten. They brought in the men who had all been beaten. They were barefoot- their shoes had been taken. It hurt so much to see my son there. They kept bringing more men in and then beating and kicking them.

The police kept shouting vulgarities at them. I saw one of my nephews there too and thought, "Oh my God, it's another one of my family members…" My nephew studies at the Technology Institute. It was awful to see family members there, beaten. After all the men entered and they had us all there, the police officers would say, "Careful not to move, you hear?" And they had us like that, our hands and our feet tucked underneath us. We were so tired and they kept telling us not to move. They laughed at us and joked around amongst themselves and finally I heard them say, "All right then, load up this truck. Men first."

And they started to make the men stand up, twisting their hands painfully, pulling them by the hair and punching them from behind. I thought that they were going to kill us, I was so scared.

I'm 50 years old and never ever had I ever seen anything like this. I kept telling myself, "I think they're going to kill me." They started to take out the men and I saw how they brought my family members and all the other men that were there. It hurt me so much to see them there. I thought to myself, "This is where they're going to kill us". You could hear a lot of noise in the distance and I heard them whistle. I began to imagine the worst for my family and for the men…

About half an hour after they took the men away, then they took the women. They tied us up again from behind and pressed our heads down so that we couldn't see where we were going. I felt like I couldn't breathe and they just kept saying, "Come on, hurry up, son of a…" and so many vulgarities. We hurried. They made us run and when we got there you could hear that they had begun to open all the doors. I thought the worst, since I had never been to such a place. They put us in a tiny room where one bed just barely fits along with a toilet and sink.

I heard the female police officers say to the male officers, "They're all yours. You can do whatever you want with them." I kept thinking the worst. My children, my family…Where were they now? They were putting women in and closing the doors. I started to pray. Everything was completely silent.

The bed was a cement block. We were so cold. I was more scared than cold, though. I think it was the fear that caused me to tremble so much. I prayed that God would be with me that night.

When a policeman came back, I asked him, "Listen, do you have a blanket you could give me, it's so cold." And the policeman said, "I don't know, I'm going to try to get one, we'll see if I find one." The woman who was with me said, "Please, because it's so cold. We're going to freeze to death. Please bring one." She was crying. The policeman left and didn't return until the next day.

Later that night you could hear the men screaming nearby. I thought about my family members who were there yelling, beaten.

Finally the next day, around two or three in the afternoon, they took us out of the cells. We hadn't eaten anything or drunk any water. They didn't give us anything at all, and I was very hungry and thirsty. They took us out, saying, "Come on, we're going to take you all to the doctor," so that's where they took us. There were a lot of women who were beaten. I had two bruises but there was no blood. My bruises were swollen and everything hurt, but that was all. Some of the other women had head injuries and others had wounded hands. The women had been badly beaten.

The doctors checked us, but didn't ask us how we were or what they had done to us. Just: "How was the march?" I told them, "I don't know what you're talking about. I don't know anything about a march." And he just asked me again, "How was the march? You all were there making a big mess of things yesterday." And I said, "Doctor, did they bring me here for you to cure me or to investigate what I did or didn't do?" One doctor asked me, "Where did they hit you?" I showed them the bruises and welts. She asked, "They didn't hit you in the head did they?" "No," I told her. The doctor then said to the other doctors, "This woman doesn't have anything wrong with her. She can go, call in the next one." All the women had their turns.

When all the women were leaving the doctors' office—that's when I saw my sister. I felt terrible seeing my sister there because she had been beaten. I thought how so much of my family was there and wondered what was happening. My sister was there because she had gone out to buy school supplies for her children.

After the doctors' office, they took us back to the same place where we had already been—a big house—where they finally gave us food. It must have been four or five in the afternoon by that time. "Hurry up because we have other things to do," the police told us as we ate. Then they put us in the cells again and left.

When night came, they came again to get us, saying, "Let's go, because the public minister has arrived and you're all going to testify about the damage you've done." They took us somewhere in the same building but far from the cells, and I could see my son and my nephew. All of them had been beaten, and they made them testify. Later the women had to testify and that's where we spent the night. It was cold, and we had to spend the night there because there were so many of us. It took them forever before they finished with all of us.

It was around 5am, because it was still dark outside, when they started lining up the men. They had already taken them back up to their cells, and they started to bring them back down, four or eight at a time. They started tying them up with some kind of white plastic that cuts into the skin, and when I saw how they were tying people up and seeing my family members there, I thought, "My God, where are they going to take us? What are they going to do to us?" The police were heavily armed with huge rifles that made me so scared. They wore bulletproof vests and pushed us with the point of the rifle, saying, "Come on, walk."

When they finished with the men, they started with the women. "Now it's your turn," they told us. It occurred to me to ask one of the female police officers, "Miss, where are you going to take us? Please tell us because my family doesn't know where I am, I just want to know where you're going to take us." But she replied, "I don't have the slightest idea where they're taking you. The only thing you have to do is obey orders and don't ask questions!"

Then they began to tie up the women, pushing us with their rifles. "Don't lift your face," they said to us. I was able to see the bus—it was blue with orange stripes. They put us on the bus and there were all the poor men with their heads down hunched behind the seats. The policemen filled the aisle of the bus. We wanted to see where we were going, but they closed the curtains of the windows. It took a long time to get to wherever we were going, and when they got us off the bus we could see a huge airplane.

They lined us up again and they had us there for about two hours before they put us on the plane. The sun was high in the sky; it was warming up. They began with the men- all of whom had been beaten. They were already tied up, but this time they put iron handcuffs on them- from their wrists connected to their ankles with a chain. I could see how they were taking my son and little nephew. I felt sick. I thought it was the end of us.

Before getting on the airplane, there were so many cameras. All the police were in uniform then and one was wearing a ski mask. He held his camera saying, "Shout your number!" and said vulgar things to us. The men stated their names, addresses, and ages. After they had gotten the men onto the plane, they did the same thing with the women- taking photos, videotaping, asking us our age, where we lived, where we were born and everything. Then they put us on the airplane while they talked amongst themselves and signaled to each other.

I was terrified. When we were in the airplane, if we moved even just a little, they would poke us with their rifles, telling us not to move. I don't know how long it was before we landed.

When they got us off the airplane, they separated the men from the women. I worried about the men a lot. They put all the women on a bus. We went through a dark tunnel. It was dark when we got off the bus and you could hear lots of barking dogs and police began to yell at us, "Come on, old ladies, hurry up, run. Undress. Take off all your clothes. Hurry up, you're not at a party here."

They took our clothes away along with everything else we had and they gave us the uniforms of prisoners. We changed quickly. The police kept saying vulgar things. They brought us to our cell, with our heads down so we couldn't see. They put us in cells and brought us something to eat.

In that jail, they started giving us food and they stopped beating us. They passed each day to give us food and we had to eat there in our cells. They gave us food three times a day. They didn't ever stop shouting at us, each time they passed our cells they yelled something, but that was it.

We were there, at the prison in Nayarit, for twenty-one days. During those twenty-one days, we never heard anything about the men or about the rest of our family.

Then one day they told us that we had to go sign something because we were going to be released. They got us up around 1am and the police told us, "Give me your blanket, sheets, everything that you used. You can't leave anything for the women who are staying behind." I put all the things I had used together and they brought us down. We turned in the things we had used and they took photos of us. They counted the scars that we had. They took fingerprints, photos, videos.

In our cell, we had to leave three women who were still going to be held there. They were young women from

Huajuapan. They make those straw fans that you use to fan the fire. That's what they do for a living. One of their husbands works construction, the other two are widows. They don't have husbands anymore but they have eight, five, and three small children respectively. All of their children are less than ten years old. The women didn't know how their children were because they said that they had come into the city to run errands. They were getting ready to go back to their villages when the police arrested them.

They were crying and begging us not to go. It was so terrible to leave them there, poor things, because we know how it feels. It hurt so much to have to leave those women behind because their children and families don't know anything about them. Those women don't know how their children are and they're so worried.

That's what I lived through. The first day, when they arrested me—the police and the gases—that was the most terrible day because I didn't understand what was happening. But all twenty-one days were awful.

I never went to the marches before, but now after what the government has done to me, I'll be there to show my support. I don't know what the APPO is because I've never been to anything that has to do with the APPO, but now I'm going to support them. I've heard of the teachers and I'll support them too, now, because it hurt so much what the government did to me. They not only made me suffer, but they made my whole family suffer.

The police kept telling me that I'm part of the APPO, that I went to the march and that I visit the *plantón*. Now I really will go anywhere, to whatever march, until they release all those young women from that jail. It hurt so much to leave them there. They're so innocent, they had no idea why they were brought there, and some didn't know how to speak Spanish, just Mixteco.

I didn't support any organization before, but now I'm going to because I want all this to be over. I'll join them to get rid of this governor. Ulises should resign because I can't stand any of this. I can't bear to think of that man. I've only seen him in photos, but I don't even want to see him in photos anymore—I can't stand him.

I want to fight for the release of all the innocent women who are still in Nayarit. They are humble people.

I will work with people who have been struggling, with whichever organization, the APPO or whatever. I don't want my grandchildren to suffer what I have suffered.

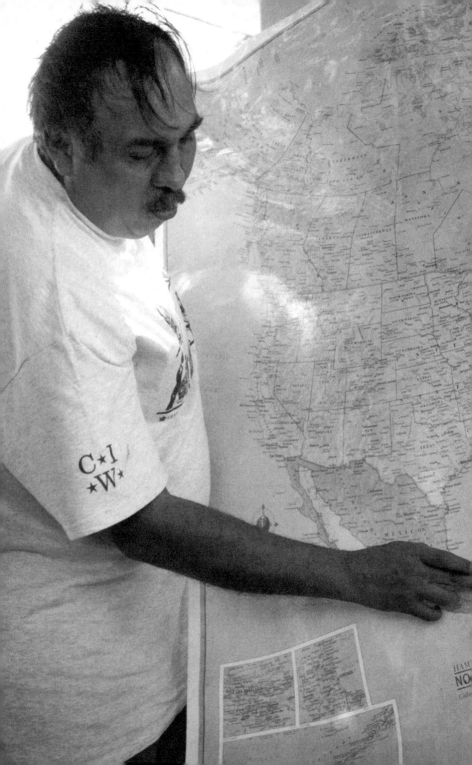

CARLOS

As many long-time activists assure us, the eviction of the teachers was merely the straw that broke the camel's back. Exploitation and repression in a single-party system was nothing new to Oaxacans, especially not to indigenous communities who have found themselves increasingly marginalized for hundreds of years. Carlos Beas, among the founders of UCIZONI, the Union of Indigenous Communities of the Northern Zone of the Isthmus, organizes the resistance of these communities to exploitative mega-development projects such as Plan Puebla Panamá. UCIZONI has been one of the most important mobilizing bodies on the isthmus and has been a key force in uniting urban and rural movements.

I'm a barefoot economist.

I say that because I've dedicated my entire life to work with indigenous communities. My personal mission is to challenge the abuses of the powerful and to organize the people in resistance to the government and large companies.

I'm over fifty now, but I've been interested in social struggle since I was a kid. I cried when I found out about the mass murder of students on October 2, 1968. It was around that time when I started reading about the life of the inexhaustible social activist of Oaxacan origin, Ricardo Flores Magón. His ideas have marked me for life. It's because of him that I believe in the self-organization of communities and not in political parties.

I studied economics at the UNAM, but I never liked the world of academia. I decided it was better to follow the struggles of independent unions and peasant and indigenous organizations. I wasn't even twenty years old when, as a result of my involvement, I was kidnapped by a paramilitary group and locked up in a clandestine prison. I was terrified, of course. I thought they were going to kill me, but I believe that in the end, the experience made me stronger.

In the 1970s, I participated in what we called the Collective Regeneration, which published a newspaper by the same name, and I also accompanied land occupations and radical strikes in different places in Mexico. We were a persecuted group and, in 1978, I had to leave the country. Outside of Mexico, I worked to promote actions for the freedom of political prisoners, and I was able to get to know activists in Europe and in the U.S.

Later I returned to Mexico and came to live on the Isthmus of Tehuantepec, where more than 25 years ago, we created a small group of teachers, indigenous people, community leaders and professionals: this collective of activists was called El Nahual; the nahual in indigenous culture refers to the animal or natural element that accompanies and protects a person throughout her life.

El Nahual was a clandestine group that met by night, because in those times there was a lot of corrupt leadership in indigenous communities. The powerful had hit men, *pistoleros*, who assassinated and threatened their opposition. *El Nahual* also was the name of the magazine that we published, in which we denounced the abuses of the government and the rich landowners. We called on the communities to organize themselves and fight back against the abuses.

In 1985 we formed UCIZONI—the Union of Indigenous Communities of the Northern Zone of the Isthmus—by bringing together the community assemblies in the region. At the beginning there were only a handful of people from eleven communities, but as the years passed, UCIZONI continued to grow and now includes more than 100 communities in Oaxaca and Veracruz.

UCIZONI organizes in resistance to landowners, large

companies, and the forest industry. UCIZONI's struggle has always been against the expropriation of lands and forests and in defense of the human rights of our indigenous people. We've organized corn and coffee cooperatives and built schools, roads and clinics.

The first years of the organization were extremely difficult because neither the government nor the powerful local strongholds of the PRI wanted communities to organize themselves independently. We had barely begun to walk when they threw the Mixe leader Armando Agustín Bonifacio in jail. Armando was someone like Chico Mendes because he defended the forests that belonged to our communities. The local leaders sent in *pistoleros* to kill him in 1995.

The eighties were difficult times in our region. An indigenous teacher who called people to struggle was stoned to death. Other people who defended themselves against the abuses of the corrupt local leader called The Tiger were assassinated or run out of their villages. Despite all odds against us, the organization grew because the villages were tired of so much injustice. This repression caused our organization to grow because the villages were tired of so much injustice.

Around 1989, UCIZONI confronted the human rights violations committed by the military, which resulted in persecution and harassment. In that period, our offices, located in the city of Matías Romero, Oaxaca, were broken into by soldiers and some of our members had to flee. Because of the aggression, UCIZONI called for the International Forum of Human Rights of the Indigenous Peoples. More than a thousand delegates attended from many parts of Mexico and seven other countries. This meeting was very important because it got together, for the first time, the organizations and *pueblos* which, in that period, had been fighting in isolation. At that forum, the Mexican council "500 Years of Indigenous, Black, and Popular Resistance" was formed, which in coming years would carry out huge mobilizations.

In 1992, hundreds of men and women of UCIZONI walked more than 600 kilometers to Mexico City to demand that the Mexican government respect the rights of the indigenous *pueblos*. We faced hunger, sickness and fatigue, but we maintained our spirit of solidarity and returned home with our heads held high.

With the Zapatista uprising in 1994, our *pueblos* mobilized immediately. Military convoys sent to attack our indigenous brothers and sisters crossed the railways and highways of our region daily. That's why on January 9, 1994, UCIZONI created a roadblock to impede the military's advance to Chiapas and to demand a peaceful and just solution to their struggle.

When the military attacked Zapatista communities in February 1995, UCIZONI sent a commission with food and clothing to Las Cañadas de Chiapas. I was sent to a small community called Nueva Estrella where military men were causing all kinds of terrible destruction. They would defecate and throw detergent and diesel over the corn fields and even killed an indigenous man. I remember seeing a young man in the village cry when the soldiers crushed his guitar.

During that period, the Zapatistas invited me to be an advisor on Agrarian Issues, so that's how I participated in the Dialogues of San Andrés de los Pobres.

In 1996, during Zedillo's presidency, the administration announced its intention to carry out a series of mega-projects in the Isthmus. It was a program of investments that included the creation of shrimp farms, monocropping plantations non-native species like eucalyptus and African palm, and the modernization of the communications and energy infrastructure. We immediately organized to inform the *pueblos*. We held many meetings and edited educational materials. We were able to stop the financial monster, and the impacts of this mega-project in our region were reduced. But a new wave would come, bigger and more powerful.

In 1998 we founded the Ricardo Flores Magón Indigenous Popular Council of Oaxaca. During almost two years we mobilized intensively because the government had unleashed an intense wave of repression against the indigenous movement. Several of the activists of the council were thrown in jail and I was in hiding for awhile, until I had to leave the country for several months. Thanks to the mobilization of the women of UCIZONI and other organizations, the prisoners were freed.

At the end of 2000, Vicente Fox had just become president when he announced a new mega-project, which he would later call *Plan Puebla Panamá*. Towards the end of February 2001, when the Zapatista *comandancia* carried out the March of the Color of the Earth, we met with Subcomandante Marcos in the pueblo on the isthmus, La Ventosa. And that's when we first resolved to resist the abuses and organized the campaign "The Isthmus is Not for Sale."

That's the year we started organizing to confront this new mega-threat. We carried out a major campaign to promote resistance. We produced videos and publications and held many informative meetings. This effort worked because the Chontal communities were able to stop the construction of the highway that would go from the Isthmus to Huatulco. But in other places, the resistance of the *pueblos* was isolated, therefore quickly defeated. The oldest and biggest organization in the region, the

Worker-Student-Peasant Coalition, was very combative during many years, but had at that time abandoned the struggle for social justice. The members were self-interested and they abandoned the *pueblos*, which did a great deal of damage in the *pueblos* by disorganizing and discouraging them.

While the government imposed its mega-project, the economic crisis seriously affected our *pueblos*, as the price of coffee and oranges had dropped drastically, and the corn market had been invaded by imports of terrible quality, cheap yellow corn. The North American Free Trade Agreement (NAFTA) seriously damaged the small producers, peasants and cattle herders, and there was a lot of migration to the North. Many families were destroyed and diseases of poverty like tuberculosis reappeared, as well as other sicknesses like diabetes.

Besides that, there continued to be a lot of corruption and all kinds of human rights violations. The governors of the PRI only appl public resources to buy votes and to make themselves rich. That situation became even more serious with Governor Ulises Ruiz. He despised UCIZONI from the beginning because in our region we were able to defeat him even though he won the elections for governor by fraud.

Ulises Ruiz, from the very beginning, was repressive. We found out how he threw people in jail from Lalana, Xanica and San Blas Atempa, just for demanding that the community leaders be respected. UCIZONI demanded the freedom of political prisoners. In early 2006, when we went to Oaxaca City to state our demands with a big commission formed by more than 250 representatives of communities where UCIZONI works, we were surrounded by hundreds of police and immobilized. But in spite of that, we were able to seize public offices.

That's why on June 14, 2006, when we found out that the

police had violently displaced a teachers' sit-in, we immediately made our voice heard and we organized to block a major highway to demand an end to the repression. UCIZONI sent a commission to the city of Oaxaca, which participated in the creation of the Popular Assembly of the Peoples of Oaxaca, the APPO.

In UCIZONI we understood that the fall of this terrible government was the beginning of a necessary democratization of public life in Oaxaca. With the fall of the PRI governor, we would be able to implement public policies that would address the needs of the poor, women and indigenous people. We knew the public offices and the courts were filled with inept and corrupt civil servants and that finally we would be able to make human rights a reality in the state. That meant for us that Ulises Ruiz had to go.

So that's why UCIZONI had actively participated in the whole movement. We had an encampment in the *plantón* in the *zócalo* in Oaxaca City. And, through our network of community radios, we kept the *pueblos* informed about what was happening in the city. We shut down the offices of the government for months. We held assemblies, organized roadblocks and blocked highways on at least 15 occasions. We organized for communities to participate in every mega-march held in the capital of Oaxaca. After finishing a march with our feet destroyed from walking over hot pavement all day, we always returned to the Isthmus with our spirits high. What was never lacking was the enthusiasm and fervor of the people; we were strengthened by the thousands of people who applauded and supported us with food and water as we walked through the streets.

The resistance of the neighborhoods in the city of Oaxaca was impressive and that's what motivated us and gave us proof of the incredible courage of the movement. The atmosphere of tension, fear, anger, and also the camaraderie that we found at the *plantón* in the *zócalo* and at the barricades made us understand that, far beyond the organizations and the APPO, the people themselves were furious and fed up with centuries of abuse and exclusion.

The great movement that took shape in the city of Oaxaca was animated by the people from the poorest neighborhoods and areas of the city, many of them migrants and indigenous people from the countryside whose poverty had brought them to the city where they now find themselves working the most difficult and poorly paid jobs.

UCIZONI helped create the APPO-Isthmus, the Assembly of the Pueblos which included students from Ixtepec, indigenous people from Guichicovi and San Blas Atempa, some teachers of Section XXII of the Teachers Union, peasants from Tehuantepec and neighbors from Matías Romero and Salina Cruz. Together we organized mobilizations in different places.

However, in this movement, the isthmus has been looked down upon because the organization the Coalition of Workers, Farmers and Students (COCEI) and the municipal president of Juchitán who belongs to the PRD, supported Ulises Ruiz, which is considered a serious betrayal. The role of the isthmus teachers has been questioned also, because almost from the beginning they wanted to stop organizing mobilizations. The weak and betraying attitude always bothered us, and even more when we saw how thousands of teachers from other regions fought and suffered.

UCIZONI stood strong, even on the terrible 25th November of 2006. I was in a meeting in southern Veracruz that day when I found out about the brutal repression. A group of men and women from our organization participated in the mobilization that was so repressed. We could hear the screams and cries of our *compañeros* in the background when they called us from the march.

On November 26th, with the support of our *compañeros* and *compañeras* from Veracruz, we took over a commercial radio in Minatitlán and from the microphones of Radio Wolf, we denounced the police brutality in Oaxaca, and later we blocked the highway. That same night, the police organized repressive operations there.

On December 10, 2006 when the subsiding of the movement was evident, the *pueblos* of the Isthmus once again blocked the transnational highway, demanding the freedom of our political prisoners. That mobilization brought us further repression. Almost immediately police checkpoints were set up and they intensified vigilance around our homes. According to the declarations of the federal police last December, the town of Matías Romero, Oaxaca remained a stronghold of the resistance.

In UCIZONI, we don't only struggle against corrupt governments. During these same months, we maintained our struggle against the imposition of mega-projects underway on the isthmus. We motivated the creation of the Indigenous Community Radios of the Isthmus as well as the Pueblos of the Isthmus in Defense of Lands, which is fighting against the mass windmill construction in the isthmus that is supported by the World Bank, USAID and Spanish companies such as Iberdrola. We also organized in response to the environmental impacts provoked by the oil company PEMEX in our region. That is to say, we have many points of attack against the brutal neo-liberal offensive.

I ended 2006 tired and sick, just like a lot of *compañeros*. In 2007 I had to have surgery, which allowed me to rest a couple of days, but soon I returned to my activities and I'm enthusiastic and very active, preparing new actions, writing a book, participating in new struggles, and expecting a baby girl who will be born soon.

I know that there are still *compañeros* and *compañeras* who are in jail. I know that we haven't been able to expel the huge corporations from these lands and that this repressive governor keeps provoking suffering in the people. There is a lot to fight for. I know that this struggle continues and that our resolve and determination will last as long as God and the body allow it to. *La lucha sigue*. The struggle continues, Oaxaca. *Salud*.

JENNY

When American independent journalist Brad Will was murdered at a barricade on October 27, 2006, the world's attention turned to the uprising in Oaxaca and the government repression that had already taken the lives of twenty-six other Oaxacan activists. The state attorney general, who (as in many countries around the world) is mostly concerned with political maneuverings—and entirely subordinate to the state governor's orders—manipulated evidence to hold movement activists, rather than government-contracted paramilitary forces, responsible for the murder. Brad's family visited Oaxaca to demand that the case be tried in federal courts, and to demand justice, not only for their son, but also for all the victims of the repression. Jenny, an international human rights observer, accompanied the family during their meetings with government officials, the reenactment of their son's assassination, a memorial march for assassinated activists, and visits with other families who lost loved ones as a result of the violent repression.

The dates March 23—25th 2007 have been circled on my calendar for weeks. They mark the days that Brad Will's family will be in Oaxaca. I never met the Indymedia journalist, I arrived in Oaxaca just days after he was killed, but his death and his family's visit affect my life in many ways. Of the five witnesses that will be testifying in front of the Federal Attorney General on behalf of the family, some are my friends, and another, the only family I have here in Oaxaca. All five of these witnesses are aware of the danger they face in testifying; the events of this past year in Oaxaca have left little doubt as to the danger one faces when speaking out against the state government. Each witness has been subjected to harassment and intimidation by various government agents—one witness was forced into hiding—and their houses are under constant surveillance, yet they are all willing to take the risk now, and they do it in honor and in memory of Brad.

I have never met the Will family, but I am imagining the trauma they will go through during their visit here. Like them, I am a foreigner here in Mexico, like them I come from a place where conceptions and expectations of responsible government, the law and the justice system are different. I come from a country where death isn't quite so common, where faith isn't quite as strong, and the everyday horrors that people face in Mexico are merely images we see on the television. Our ability to cope, our ability to understand the death of a child, the death of a son, a daughter, a sister, a brother, are distinct, only because government sanctioned assassinations aren't nearly as common in our countries. Without living in Mexico, there is no context for us to understand the system here, at least for the privileged classes of Northern countries. This is a system where corrupt politicians are able to manipulate investigations, and state attorneys build cases around hypotheses aimed only at absolving the state of any wrongdoing.

So I am worried, because at this point, I'm not sure just how much of the state prosecutor's story Brad's family believe, or how much, for that matter, they believe the stories in the press. All I know is that they are coming to demand a just and impartial investigation into their son's murder and to ensure that those responsible for his death are held accountable. I can only continue to hope that the compassion and the integrity their son displayed here in Oaxaca is a reflection of the kind of people they are.

On March 21st, we are scheduled to have a private meeting among the witnesses, the family, the lawyers and the translators, before retracing Brad's last steps from the Calicanto Barricade.

When the day finally arrives, we set up the video cameras and the audio equipment under the shadow of 27 black crosses, painted with the names of the 27 fallen activists who have died during the ten-month struggle. In the center of the room, the cross that reads Bradley Roland Will has two red flowers tied under his name. No one is speaking very much, just sitting quietly on the wooden benches arranged in a semicircle. We wait.

And then the moment finally arrives. Brad's parents, Kathy and Hardy, along with their eldest son, Craig, walk across the yard accompanied by their lawyer and their translator. Everyone stands and Kathy bursts into tears. Here in front of her stand five people, I'm sure the family have seen their faces a hundred times in videos, on the news, in the newspapers, but now they are here in the flesh, five people who tried to save the life of their son and now stand accused of his murder. I can only imagine the depths of their grief and anger…After a few moments, the Wills recover their composure and those present begin introducing themselves. When it is Hardy's turn, he does not speak. Instead he strides across the room to embrace those who tried to help his son and whispers, "Thank you, thank you for all you tried to do." We all breathe a sigh of relief and the meeting begins. Each witness is meant to recount their experience of the day Brad died and give the family a chance to ask any questions. That's it. The meeting is scheduled to last two hours. But one thing you learn quickly in Mexico is that nothing ever goes according to plan.

As the witnesses begin to speak, other people start arriving: faces I recognize from the barricades and from the marches, from photographs and from the videos shot on November 2nd, 20th, and 25th. These are the people who were on the front lines during the most intense moments of the conflict, and they have all come to pay their respects to the Will family. As the testimonies begin so, too, begin the personal stories about Brad. The respect and love these people have for him is more than evident. Amidst the tears there is laughter, amidst the tears there is warmth, a breaking down of barriers between strangers, between languages and between cultures.

It is this phenomenon that is Brad's legacy. His ability, as a foreigner, in one short month, to win the hearts of an entire movement. He won peoples' trust and their respect, and, over and over again, this morning I hear testaments to his strength, his courage, his professionalism, and above all else, his humanity, his humility and his solidarity. And then it is the family's turn to speak, but by now all formalities have been cast aside. Kathy thanks everyone for being there. She acknowledges the danger the witnesses face and she promises to help them in any way she can. They have traveled a long way, she says, and more than meetings with government officials and chief prosecutors, these are the people she has come to Oaxaca to meet, because these are the people who ensured that her son did not die alone. She is so grateful to these people, she explains, because in the darkest days of their grief, the one comforting thought she and her family had was that Brad died surrounded by love, in the arms of his friends, in the arms of the people he had come to Oaxaca to fight for.

And then it is time to go. The press is waiting and members of APPO and VOCAL and others from the barricades have organized a march to accompany the family on the difficult journey through the streets of Santa Lucía. The media close in, desperate for the classic shot of the grieving parents and to record the perfect 15-second sound bite that will make the 10:30 news. Once they've got it, they disappear and we continue on through the streets. Brad's mom is telling childhood stories about her son to the translators, people are holding up their words of support on fluorescent colored posters and they are chanting "*Brad no Murió, Ulises lo Mató*" (Brad didn't die, Ulises killed him).

We walk together, 27 black crosses—each representing an assassinated activist—leading the way. And although the tensions of the morning have dissipated, everyone is aware that we are walking in a dangerous neighborhood, a PRI stronghold, and the marchers are vulnerable. Two police motorcycles have been spotted on either side of us, just close enough for us to know they are there, but we continue on. Kathy, Hardy and Craig want to lay flowers at the site where Brad fell but when we arrive we find that the cross and the vigil that marks the spot have been stolen sometime earlier in the morning. It has happened before, but no one guessed that it could happen today. The march pauses briefly and then as we turn the corner nearing the end of our walk, two municipal police pickups appear before us. There are at least eight officers. Some are carrying high-powered rifles. As we watch them try and detain a middle-aged man, fear turns to anger and members of the independent media move in. With cameras and microphones shoved in their faces, the police quickly release the man and defend their presence on the street by saying that they are there to protect the children getting out of school for the day. There is nothing more to do. This form of intimidation is nothing new and we return once again to the family, determined to continue on with the day's events.

When we arrive back at the house, we learn that Brad's parents and his brother Craig have cancelled their next press conference. They want to stay to have more time with those who have risked the journey into Santa Lucía to meet them. Brad's mom is presented with her son's missing tennis shoe—the only personal belonging that had not been returned to the family after his death. It had been placed on his shrine here in Oaxaca and then safeguarded until the day his friends could return it to his parents in person. But it is not only Brad's friends who have arrived to speak with Kathy, Hardy and Craig. Widows and mothers of the other dead activists are here too and they begin their introductions by acknowledging their shared pain and loss. As the women hug one widow says simply, "You are a part of our family now."

This pain cuts across all cultural barriers, it crosses all borders. But as Kathy sits with these proud, strong women, the differences between them are also clear. While the Wills are in Mexico fighting for a federal investigation into their son's murder, these women know that there is little chance that anyone will investigate the assassinations of their husbands and sons. To date not one other case has been opened. "How sad," says one widow, "that it takes a foreigner to die before anyone will pay attention to the injustices we face."

It is a feeling I have been struggling with for some time. Because although the Will family has tirelessly and emphatically stated in each and every press conference that they are not only demanding justice for their son, but also for all the assassinated, the disappeared and the tortured, I wonder just how many people know the other names: Emilio Alonso Fabian, José Alberto Lopez Bernal, Fidel Sanchez Garcia, and Esteban Zurita Lopez—the other victims assassinated here in the city the very same week. Why did it take the death of an American journalist before anyone paid attention? But I banish those thoughts for another day because I find it more inspiring to watch these women exchange hugs and tears and email addresses, and when

the day finally ends, I feel nothing but gratitude for having witnessed such a powerful reunion.

The next day, we wake up early and all the warm feelings of the day before seem far away. Today we enter into the belly of the beast; today the five witnesses will testify in front of the Federal Attorney General. We arrive before 9:00am and meet with Brad's family once again. The 27 crosses stand against the green steel fence that encloses the federal building in San Bartolo Coyotepec. There are about 50 people here to support the witnesses and continue their demands for justice in the other 26 cases using flags and banners, words and a hunger strike to pressure the government and to attract media attention. For this, they are subjected to a day of intimidation tactics taken straight out of some Hollywood movie. There are police officers walking around, helicopters flying overhead, plainclothes cops driving up and down the dead end street.

We watch the federal police patrolling the front entrance; they pass through the gate periodically to take our pictures and videotape us. Throughout the day, a number of unmarked cars park in front of us, reminding us that there is always a price to pay for non-conformity. But perhaps the most frustrating aspect of the day is the constant delays from inside the Attorney General's office. By four o'clock, only one witness has finished testifying and everyone is nervous. At one point, the witnesses ask the Wills' lawyer to seek some kind of protection for them and for those outside, but the family is all but powerless to do much. The two parties talk and once again those testifying agree to enter the building. I ask one of them why. Why are you risking your lives? And he simply replies, because it is the right thing to do and it is our way to pay homage to our friend and our brother. It is a sentiment shared by all who have come with their cards and their flowers, their poems and their stories of an idealistic activist who gave his life trying to give voice to their cause.

When the last witness exits the building, it is 11:00pm and we quietly make our way home, weary from the 15 hours of surveillance and press conferences. The Wills are tired, too, but they are jubilant. Eleven cases, including that of their son, have been taken out of the hands of the state attorney. In the press conference, they reiterate that the state hypothesis that Brad was shot at close range by protesters and then shot again in transit to the Red Cross was "ridiculous, false, without substance, biased and unconvincing" and repeated their conviction that state attorney Lizbeth Caña Cadeza acted in bad faith, altering evidence in order to clear the state of any responsibility and to protect government paramilitary assassins. Kathy and Hardy have cancelled their flight in order to watch the beginnings of the federal investigation into their son's death, an investigation they hope will finally lead to justice. The witnesses have been subpoenaed to be back at the scene of the crime tomorrow.

And so the federal investigation begins at 11:00am on the 23rd of March. Men and women in white lab coats begin stretching yellow ribbon across the infamous streets of Santa Lucia del Camino. They plan to re-enact the events of October 27, 2006, step by step, measurement by measurement. The people supporting the family and the witnesses are here once again and the press has arrived on schedule. The show begins and I can only sit and wait. I make mental notes of the photographers I have never seen before, faces in the crowd that I do not recognize and I sit with Brad's mom as she takes out the family photographs she has been carrying around with her since the day she arrived in Mexico.

There are pictures of family vacations, ski trips, weddings, pictures of Brad with his nieces and nephews—he looks like a typical American boy from a typical middle-class American family, if not for the fact that in nearly every picture he can be seen wearing a T-shirt supporting some social movement or another. It is hard to miss the red left fist blazoned across his chest.

I am distracted from the volunteers carrying a man down the street, a man the size and stature of Brad Will, because a little girl has approached us with a card she has made for Brad's mom. It is a picture with flowers and a sun and it says, "Brad was a friend of APPO," and I watch Kathy change from a grieving mother into a role she knows well, a grade school teacher from Illinois. Suddenly it is easy to imagine Brad's life growing up.

It is clear that at the end of the day, Kathy and Hardy are hopeful. Their faith that this new investigation will finally bring justice for their son is more than evident. In their final press conference, they thank the people of Oaxaca for all the support they have shown, and Kathy once again demands witness protection for all those who risked their lives to testify yesterday. And then we are off to share one last meal before Brad's parents head back to Mexico City.

There is nothing quite like the feeling you get sitting at a long table surrounded by friends, tortillas and *mole*. In three short days, there is no denying the bond that has formed among the people here. The sadness and loss is temporarily pushed aside and we laugh over shared experiences. What is also clear is that the Wills are not going to go home and forget the people of Oaxaca. They want to continue their fight until justice has been served—not only for their son but for the people he dedicated his life to help.

If you log on to Bradwill.org you will find that a foundation has been set up in his name. Its mission is to support and contribute to non-violent groups dedicated to the advancement of underserved people and communities throughout the world. I think it is a testament as to how the Will family sees the people of Oaxaca and of their dedication to further their son's vision of making this world a better place.

And for my part, I leave this experience feeling privileged to have met this brave and loving family and to have shared in the stories of an independent journalist and poet who helped bring the world's attention to a grassroots struggle for freedom and democracy in Oaxaca.

DAVID

In the wake of November's massive police attacks, the government began to carry out selective repression, arresting particularly vocal, visible activists and attempting to discredit them through criminal, rather than movement-related charges. David Venegas Reyes, an agronomist and activist from Oaxaca City, has been held in Ixcotel penitentiary, illegally and under false charges, since April 13, 2007. David recognizes that he was targeted not only because of his criticism and activism against the state government, but also because of his uncompromising commitment to refuse to participate in processes that legitimate state power, such as negotiations and elections, which put him in conflict with more moderate or opportunist sectors within the APPO. David discusses divisions and tensions within the APPO, and the consequent creation of Oaxacan Voices Constructing Liberty and Autonomy (VOCAL).

At first the physical space of the struggle for the people of Oaxaca was somewhat limited. The *plantón* was made up of teachers and people from political organizations. Others participated in the movement by attending marches that the teachers' union coordinated, bringing food to the *plantón* and government buildings occupied by teachers and the APPO, and by speaking on the radio. But we saw an evolution from people acting in solidarity with the teachers and as sympathizers of the APPO to people actually taking independent actions based on their own convictions and ideas about social mobilization.

Oaxaca isn't the only place where radio has played a central role in the mobilization of the people, but here, in particular, the effects of popular media control and the struggle to maintain it is impossible to underestimate. And the story of the radios in Oaxaca, is, of course, intimately linked to the history of the barricades. *Radio Plantón*, which belonged to the teachers, was lost as a result of the violent police attacks on June 14th. In July, *Radio Universidad*, property of university students, was destroyed for the first time when infiltrators poured acid on the control deck. August 21st—when police attacked and destroyed the occupied state television and radio and the people reacted by seizing twelve commercial stations by the movement—marks the birth of the barricades. Many of us took to the streets that night to seize the commercial radio stations, and when we had succeeded, we asked ourselves, "How can we defend these take-overs and protect the people inside?"

That's how the barricades were born, and that's when my participation, along with the participation of hundreds of thousands of others, began to make a more substantial difference. Because the movement stopped being defined by the announcements of events and calls for support made by the teachers' union and began to be about the physical, territorial control of communities by those communities, by way of the barricades.

Each barricade was different. There were small barricades made up of a couple of families in more remote alleyways and enormous barricades at huge intersections. Brenamiel, where I organized, falls into the latter category. It was at an important intersection in a working class part of the city. Around Brenamiel there are some of the poorest neighborhoods in the city as well as a couple of wealthier housing developments. There are no cultural centers or sports facilities or parks or anything like that. Most of us who formed the barricade were from the surrounding neighborhoods. We were women and men, small children and old people, professionals and not, and with different amounts of money in our pockets. Because it was at such an important intersection, people also came out from other parts of the city to join us.

What made the composition of the barricades interesting was that we all came together in defense. More than around one way of thinking or an ideological platform, or economic desperation, participation in the barricades, I think, was about defense. People came out to defend the social movement from the trenches of their own communities.

We originally formed the barricade to protect the antennas of *Radio Oro*, but the barricade soon took on a life of its own. You could describe it like a party, a celebration of self-governance where we were starting to make emancipation through self-determination a reality. The barricades were about struggle, confrontation, and organization. We eventually started discussing agreements and decisions made by the APPO Council and the teachers' union. There were a number of occasions when the barricade chose actions that went against those agreements, which in my view, only strengthened our capacity for organized resistance.

In this way, the barricades reestablished and modified the social fabric of the neighborhoods, of the communities where they were. Our relationships to our neighbors changed. Many people who we considered our friends or imagined we had things in common with weren't there, while other people who we hadn't spoken to before or hadn't had voice in the neighborhood were active in the barricades. So at the barricades we formed new networks, new friendships, and new relationships of trust in our own communities. That's why I say that the social fabric changed through the barricades and that Oaxaca remains changed by those experiences.

Daily life, as part of the poor and exploited peoples of Mexico, has been all the political schooling I've needed to motivate my participation in this social movement and at the barricades.

I've experienced it personally and seen my family and my neighbors suffer the same exploitation—at work and otherwise—that the majority of Mexicans suffer. Also, because our teachers are so well-organized politically, just by being educated in public schools in Mexico, you get an early exposure to protests starting from the time you're in elementary school.

***

On October 9, 2006, I was named representative of the barricades to the APPO Council. There were thousands of people at that APPO Congress: 1300 representatives from all around the state—from barricades, neighborhoods, rural communities, civic associations, unions, and some people from outside the state and from other countries. Recognizing the difficulty of getting together the entire statewide assembly for constant meetings, we formed the Council to make decisions—not fundamental decisions that required the approval of the assembly, but rather, strictly circumstantial decisions; I was to represent the barricades on that Council.

However, it was around that time that the state brutality intensified. On November 25th, Vicente Fox and Ulises Ruiz joined forces to repress our people in a genocidal fashion, murdering, raping and disappearing people. Along with many other activists, I left the state for around a month. But it was clear that no one was giving up, that the struggle continued, and on December 23rd I returned to Oaxaca.

***

In February, I helped found VOCAL—Oaxacan Voices Constructing Autonomy and Liberty—because a number of *compañeros* felt the need to create a space where we could exercise our own ways of thinking, and our own activism, within the social movement. The idea stemmed from an APPO Statewide Assembly when it became evident that there were divergent perspectives with regard to the upcoming elections. One position was that the APPO movement, in all its plurality and diversity, had already made clear who was left out: political parties and any corrupt institution. So on principle, the APPO shouldn't get involved in elections, because that would necessarily attack the unity constructed from diversity of thought and visions that exist within the movement.

A second position stated that in spite of all that, we should act pragmatically and participate in the elections with our own candidates. It was a broad discussion, but after that assembly some of us called a meeting to gather people who agreed with the idea of respecting the principles on which the social movement was founded and opposed participating in the processes that serve to legitimate repressive governments. There were a lot of people who came to the meeting precisely because of their mistrust of some of the organizations within the APPO who had offered a conciliatory discourse with respect to the government. Many of the *compañeros* who formed VOCAL didn't even participate in the APPO at all, but in the broader social movement they were active and courageous.

So VOCAL turned into a diverse organization where a lot of anti-authoritarian visions and ways of thinking coexist— some rooted in indigenous tradition, like *magonismo*, and some more connected to European ideologies. A lot of *compañeros* who have no particular ideological doctrine are also active in the organization; we participate in the social movement and in the struggle that takes place in the street.

What we all have in common is our idea of autonomy as a founding principle. We defend the diverse ways of organizing of *pueblos* and the rights of people to self-govern in all realms of life. We believe in autonomy as a political proposal for community as well as personal life. Unlike other hegemonic ideologies, we don't believe that to promote our own line of thought it's necessary to exclude anyone else's.

Autonomy doesn't have to raise its proud head and look down upon other ways of thinking to be able to exist. Because of the diversity within our organization as well as the diversity that we observe in Oaxaca and in the social movement, we founded our organization on this concept. The autonomy we believe in makes possible the coexistence of different forms of thought, as long as they correspond with personal and collective actions that are respectful.

We find that in Oaxaca, Mexico and Latin America, the struggles for autonomy are a constant in the landscape of insurgency, emerging—many of them—from within indigenous communities all over the continent. Many indigenous *pueblos*, as individual communities or entire regions, have risen up against the government to defend their own forms of governance and their own lifestyles. Like our Zapatista *compañeros*, for example, who rose up in 1994 against the state, and inherited a part of their discourse from the revolutionary guerrillas of Central America in the 1980's. The struggles for autonomy have always found fertile ground in indigenous *pueblos*, defining their resistance for over 500 years.

Almost all of us are indigenous or *mestizo*. We all find our ancestry in the *pueblos*, and come from the distant mountains and valleys. Personally, I see the quest for autonomy as going back to our roots, to what we've been, what we are, and what we don't want to stop being: indigenous people, children of indigenous people.

***

It's important to mention, though, that while embracing diversity, VOCAL has also had constant, real confrontations with groups and individuals in the APPO that we don't see as acting in line with the values inherent to the social movement. I've made my position clear regarding disputes within the movement and within the APPO Council as well as with respect to people who have betrayed the social movement, who have only taken advantage of the movement to benefit themselves, who have sold out, politically or economically. I've been outspoken because I think that's our responsibility. Part of our limitations and disorganization as a movement has been due to conflicts with and control by these kinds of groups. I see it as our duty to denounce and confront that kind of coop-ting. We have to have the courage to defend what's ours.

***

The monster of state terror that we saw in November never retreated. We recognized soon that the repression was here to stay, to create an atmosphere of terror to keep the people submissive. On the backdrop of that terror and in the context of movement divisions, I was arrested in April 2007. They arrested me violently with no arrest warrant or explanation. They drove me to an unknown place where they planted drugs on me, then tried to force me to hold the drugs so that they could take photos. When I refused, they beat me. After five hours, they turned me over to the federal attorney general. There they presented me with the drugs they had planted on me and kept me for two days before I was transferred to the penitentiary Santa María Ixcotel, where I remain today. Finally, they presented me with the arrest warrant that accused me of being involved in the social movement and the acts of November 25th. The warrant accused me of sedition, organized crime, and arson. Even as the government fabricated the idea of accusing me of drug possession in an attempt to criminalize and discredit me, they already intended to present the arrest warrant of a political nature once I was in jail.

Obviously, I was detained because I have a visible presence in the movement. The police, surely, knew that I was involved. But I don't think that's what distinguishes me from other *compañeros* who also actively participated in the movement. It's not so much a question of visibility, but rather, the way I acted within the movement. I always tried to be respectful of the feelings and the motivations of the *pueblos* and I didn't only confront the state and it's repression, but also moderate groups within the movement that looked for reconciliation with the government at any cost. I recognize that it was in this context that I was arrested. I was arrested by the state police, but not without the indirect collaboration of certain people in the movement who, at one point, even accused me of being a government spy. So my arrest is like so many others, *compañeros* turning in other *compañeros*. Part of it was the government and part of it had to do with the opportunists within the movement.

I received significant support and solidarity from human rights organizations nationally and internationally, which was helpful in forcing the state to drop the drug charges. For the other charges, associated with the acts of November 25th, my legal defense was successful in proving my innocence. The judge ruled that for two of the crimes I was accused of (sedition and organized crime) there's no corpus delicti; it has to be proven that a crime has occurred before a person can be convicted of committing that crime, and in this case, these crimes were determined non-existent. With respect to the only charge that actually constituted a crime, arson, I was declared not guilty.

It turns out that the Federal Public Minister appealed the case, meaning that I had to stay in jail for two more months. We won the case, which should have mandated my release from prison, but instead the government reclassified my crimes. What had been sedition, organized crime and arson have been replaced by five new crimes: attacks on communication centers, resisting arrest, dangerous attacks, crimes against government bureaucrats, and rebellion. The most serious of this diverse array of charges, without a doubt, is rebellion, which means taking up arms against the government.

Despite the fact that Ulises Ruiz Ortiz's administration has no proof whatsoever to back up these accusations, the laws in Mexico and Oaxaca permit the state to hold us in prison while they determine whether or not their accusations are true. The law in Mexico is made to benefit the powerful. We're guilty until proven innocent. I'm here on new charges, obviously false, but I'm obligated to remain in jail while we prove it.

None of this is anything new, of course. In Mexico the law is used as a form of revenge—revenge against those who challenge the government and its actions. There are around 500 political prisoners around the country, some of whom have been in jail for up to 15 years. In Oaxaca, there are still thirteen political prisoners from the Loxicha region who have been in jail, under the accusation of being guerrillas, for the last 12 years. The prisons in Mexico are full of innocent people, full of political prisoners and prisoners of conscience, and yet the federal and state governments say that there are no political prisoners. In my case in particular, the criminal and assassin Ulises Ruiz Ortiz—against whom I, personally, haven't eased my criticisms, neither outside nor inside of the prison—has used the judges and the state attorneys, in short, the entire judicial system, to keep me in jail. It's not only unjust, but also illegal, even according to the notion of legality and the legal structure on which they operate.

***

Even though I'm here in prison, I feel hopeful because I see a certain momentum and impetus in the movement of the peoples of Oaxaca. The causes of the conflict and the social movement—the injustice, violence, misery—are all still here. Nothing has changed.

Ulises Ruiz Ortiz embodies the neo-liberal model for Oaxaca, seeking to impose corporate globalization by methods already evident in Mexico and in other parts of the world. Social movements have always pointed out the advancement of exploitation, of neo-liberalism, but because of the outright treason of some movement leadership and the dispersion of activists, which is at the root of the movement's current contraction, neo-liberalism is looking to extend its tentacles into our land.

There's almost always a great resistance to these neo-liberal projects, so much so that, frequently, the only way they can be imposed is through repression and authoritarianism. We've seen that what started as repression concentrated in Oaxaca is turning into a constant around the country. As the insurgency advances and develops, so do the tactics of repression.

So many projects in Oaxaca today—mines, dams, highways—are aimed at stripping us of the resources of our communities. They divide and mutilate our lands on so many fronts. But of course, we continue to resist. I see a movement that, in spite of aggression and violence, is revitalizing.

Despite the fact that we have one of the worst, most repressive governments that we've had in Mexico for years—not to say we haven't had our share in the past also—we have hope. We have our hearts, our hands, our motivation. Those who've fallen in the movement also form part of our motivation.

The movement of the peoples of Oaxaca fell only by way of violence. The government wasn't successful in overthrowing us by lies or blackmail or betrayal even, only by outright violence were they able to break us apart.

I'm hopeful that among our *pueblos*, in our hearts—and I'm quite sure of the justice of our causes—sooner or later, we'll triumph.

After nearly a year in prison on false charges, David was released on March 5, 2008.

Ombro con omb
codo con codo
la appa, la appa,
la
apposemos todos.

DERWIN

Entire families were affected by the conflict in Oaxaca. Children saw the adults in their lives enraged and sometimes divided, and heard about their teachers who had been attacked at the plantón. Some children felt the repression even more personally. Nine-year old Derwin has been a vocal presence in the movement since his father, Marcelino Coache, an APPO spokesperson, was arrested in December. Coache, along with several other APPO spokespersons, was in Mexico City to meet for talks scheduled by the federal government. Rather than following through with negotiations, the federal government organized a police operation in which all four APPO members were arrested and tortured. Derwin's father was held in a high security prison for six months.

I'm nine years old and in fourth grade at Andrés Portillo. I really like school. My favorite subject is math, because I like counting. I also like to draw. Isidoro Garcia is my teacher. I really like him a lot because he teaches us good things like history, geography and math. He was at the *plantón*.

I had seen the *plantón* before when I stopped by with my dad. The whole center was filled with tents. Some people were drawing, others weaving and some people were reading. A *plantón* is when everyone camps out under the sun or in the rain, even at night and when it's really cold.

Not all of our teachers explained to us about the *plantón*, but I knew why they were on strike. They're demanding a minimum wage for teachers. My parents explained to me that the things some people say about the teachers aren't true. Things like that they're just looking out for their own self-interest and that they don't even know what they're fighting for. My dad explained that their struggle was for more resources for all Oaxacans.

My dad played an important role in the APPO, which is the Popular Assembly of the Peoples of Oaxaca. He is an APPO spokesperson. The APPO is a meeting, a big meeting where all the communities in Oaxaca come together. All those people got together to demand a minimum wage. They also demanded freedom for political prisoners and justice for the assassinated and disappeared. I went to about half of the meetings. There were spokespeople, activists, and teachers from the union. They talked about a lot of different things.

My dad was always going to the marches and my mom stayed home to take care of us. Before my dad was arrested, we used to receive death threats sometimes. I was the one who answered the phone for some of the phone calls that were death threats. One time, they told me, "We know your name and what school you go to and how old you are and we're going to kill you." I was sad and I gave the phone to my dad. They kept saying things to him, but he never told me what they said.

There were men who started hanging around outside our house. The day they arrested my dad, those guys were there all day, just standing there. One would go away and someone else would come back. They wouldn't leave us in peace until we went to stay at another house and closed this one up. We took everything with us; we didn't leave papers or anything inside. We felt safer in the other house.

I also remember helicopters. One day when I was with my grandma I heard a helicopter pass by really low. It was the color of the clothes that the army wears and I ran inside fast.

***

No one told me anything the day my dad was arrested; I went to bed that night and no one had told me anything. I asked about him and they just told me he was at a meeting in Mexico City. I said, "I know someone is lying to me. Someone is hiding something about my dad." My grandma, my uncle, and my whole family except my mom were there. They all said, "We're not hiding anything from you." I said, "Yes you are. You told me he was going to arrive today, so why hasn't he?" My mom finally told me that he was in Mexico City and that he had been arrested. My dad was with Flavio, Eric, Ignacio and Horacio, and they all got arrested. I yelled and was really sad. I think I had low blood pressure because I fainted that morning. While my dad was in prison I was so angry and so sad at the same time, because I just couldn't believe it. From one day to the next, he wasn't with my family anymore. I didn't want to wake up anymore. I thought, "Why should I wake up if there's no point, if my dad isn't home?"

But my mom said to me, "We have to fight to demand your father's freedom."

So that's when I started going to the marches. I made a banner that said, "I demand my father's freedom." I also wrote a letter to Santa Claus. I said, "Dear Santa, I don't want any presents for Christmas this year. What I want is for my dad to be released." They didn't release him until the 31st of May though.

I yelled many things at the marches. I demanded freedom for my dad and shouted all the slogans. I don't want to tell you all the slogans I invented because you might laugh. Things like, "Calderón, your underwear is showing!" But the slogan I invented so that they would let my dad go was, "Ulises, you dirty rat, *tlacuache*, give us back our Coache!" And I like the

slogan that goes, "*Hombro con hombro, codo con codo, la appo, la appo, la appo somos todos,*" Arm in arm, shoulder to shoulder, the APPO, the APPO, we are all the APPO. That's my favorite one because my dad invented it. I shouted all the other ones too, "Keep up the fight for a government that belongs to workers, farmers, and the people!" Also, "If Ulises won't step down, peace won't come around!" When we went to the marches and I looked over my shoulder, I saw so many people. The streets weren't even big enough to fit all those people.

At the Kilometer of Coins, people put spare change on the ground in a line trying to make a trail a whole kilometer long to raise money for political prisoners and their families. I went around asking for money to add to the trail. There were people who didn't believe me. They said, "That's not for political prisoners, you're going to keep that money." But I didn't keep any of it; I put it all into the Kilometer of Coins. One time we really did get up to a whole kilometer, but the other times we didn't quite make it.

***

When I visited my dad in jail, we had to travel six hours to Córdoba, then another hour and a half to Tezonapa and from there another half an hour to Cosolapa. I went with my mom, my little sister Luz Divina who's four and my brother Edgar who's fifteen.

The guards at the jail checked us before they let us go into the jail, to make sure we weren't carrying drugs or weapons. We brought my dad food. Sometimes tomatoes or beans, but we couldn't bring in a lot of things because the guards didn't like it. The prison was a big building, but very old. The area where people played soccer was all fenced off with barbed wire.

My dad knows how to play soccer, but with his arm dislocated, he couldn't really play. They dislocated his arms when they arrested him in Mexico City. Inside the prison there were so many people, so many men. The first time I saw my dad, I told him, "Dad, come home!" I really wanted him to be home with us. I felt so sad when he couldn't come back with us. We had to go back to Oaxaca City to go to the marches.

I kept asking to talk to the director. Once in the parking lot we were in the car of the teachers who picked us up and were about to drive away when we saw the director pull up. I got out of the car and went up to him. I said to him, "Mr. Director, my dad is not a delinquent like they say he is. He's a social activist. I don't want him to be suffering." The director said, "We're doing everything we can to take care of your father." I felt a tiny bit better, but not much.

***

On the day when my dad got out of jail, no one told me because they didn't want me to be disappointed. They had already told us he would be released the month before and we were all prepared, then they reclassified his crimes. That was terrible because we wanted to see him so much.

So I didn't know. But then they called asking if my mom was there. They told me, "The lawyer is going to come over to take care of some paperwork." There were reporters. And then Mario came over and asks me, "Coachito, what are you doing here? Didn't they tell you that your dad's on his way? Go catch up with them because they're coming." And I started running and also started crying. But crying out of happiness because I was about to see my dad again.

That first night after he was released it was almost like a march. Because the house filled up, there were at least two hundred people in this little house!

This march that I'm drawing was after my dad got out of jail. About twenty days later. These people at the march are teachers from the union and family members of political prisoners. This is me, under the tree. I'm about to join everyone to ask for freedom for the rest of the political prisoners. It's important because the families of political prisoners are really sad that a family member isn't with them.

I kept participating in the marches after my dad was released. The children's march was on April 30th. We were at the head of the march; there were at least a hundred kids there. We left from Plaza de la Danza and walked down Independencia Street, then to the *zócalo* and up to Carmen Alto. A lot of my friends were there. I have friends at school who don't know about any of this. I've tried to convince them that the PRI and the PAN are bad, but sometimes they haven't wanted to pay attention. I tell my friends, "Why should we vote for them, if they're nothing but a bunch of assassins, if they just want to kill people?" I convinced one of my friends. Now, he tells me, "You're right. What's the point of voting? From now on, I'm not going to have anything to do with the PRI or the PAN."

I still worry about my dad. On June 14th of this year, he got pulled out of his car by three policemen. They hit him in the face and took his cell phone. I was with him, but I couldn't do anything because I was afraid if I did they might arrest me too. I was so scared they would take him away again. I like having my dad at home. It makes me feel a lot better. I like it when we can take walks in the countryside. We climb up the mountain from our house and sometimes we pick wildflowers or lilies that grow up there.

It's good what my dad has done. He's defending people's rights—like being able to demand freedom and to speak about a lot of things. But the government doesn't want us to speak about anything because it's like a weapon when we speak. The government officials get angry when we talk about them.

I would like people not to be so poor. I wish people had better houses, not ones made out of tin and cardboard. I'd like better schools, too. When I grow up I want to be a dentist. To prevent people from having infections in their teeth. I've gone to the dentist and it's scary, but I want to be one anyway. My patients will be my mom, my dad, my sister and my brother. When I'm a dentist, I'll be able to help poor people too, at least in something. I'm also going to keep fighting for a better society.

Derwin's Parents Reflect

Reyna

It was hard to raise my husband's spirits and give my children strength, when sometimes I felt I didn't have any more. We took our children out of school for a period, because the threats we were receiving were so terrible. The economic situation was difficult, too. It was hard to be able to get together enough money to visit my husband who was so far away, to be able to bring him something to eat. We could only visit him every two or three weeks, maybe twelve times total in those six months. There were moments when my children had no milk to drink because we just didn't have any money at all.

I can never forgive the government for all the pain they have caused my children. They haven't gotten over the trauma of these experiences. And if my children are like this, imagine the children of the people that the government assassinated. First they feel despair, and then fear. I've seen my children so sad, so powerless sometimes because they feel like the government is a great monster that could destroy them at any moment.

But I tell my children that we can't let ourselves feel like victims or feel sorry for ourselves. We have to move forward and learn from these experiences. We have to fight this fight.

***

Coache

Prison was terrible, although it ended up being a place where I was respected. But even if a prison is made of gold, it's still a prison, because the solitude is really something terrible, you can't compare it to anything else. Even when my family would visit, it was so difficult to see my wife, my children suffer.

I think the six months I spent in that prison only helped strengthen my will to work for democracy, liberty, and justice for my people. But the freedom I want isn't just freedom from prison. I want freedom for my people. I want people to have the basic means to live, I want them to be able to speak their minds. I've always told my family and my wife that we're poor, that's obvious, but I have a job. Our income isn't much, but it comes every month. There are people a lot worse off than we are, so we have to do what we can for them. This movement has taken an important step. People have opened their eyes to the abuses, and they know that it's possible to speak out against them. There are people speaking out against the repression in their communities.

My father used to say that every human being is a leader. But there are leaders that develop, and those that are born. I believe my children have been born leaders. Derwin knows why the movement exists, and where it's going; he isn't going about it on blind faith. I know because this is something I've lived myself. In 1977 I was ten years old, and I lived through the student movement to oust then-governor Manuel Zárate Alquino with my father. Together we saw repression and death, and witnessed the growth of a movement of similar importance. This time it was Derwin's turn. It's a cycle. Just like the way we speak about the revolution of 1910- with 2010 around the corner, we're expecting the cycle to continue. But we're here on the frontlines now, and that's where we'll stay.

ADÁN

While people coordinated a united front across the state to over-throw Oaxacan governor Ulises Ruiz Ortiz, many local movements organized simultaneously to address local politics inconsistent with traditions of self-governance. Autonomous municipalities that replaced corrupt mayors with popular assemblies sprung up all over the state of Oaxaca. Zaachila is one municipality that has had success installing a people's government and radio station with widespread community support. Adán, an elementary school principal and community radio director, witnessed the mobilization of the Oaxacan town that now serves as an example to communities around the state.

Zaachila, a small city south of Oaxaca, was the cradle of the Zapotec civilization. There are approximately 25,000 residents, but now only the oldest community members speak Zapoteco. We grow corn, peanuts, and jicama, which is a fruit harvested around All Saints Day. A lot of people also raise beef cattle and hogs and many bake bread and *mole*, a spicy salsa known in the region. Fortunately, we also have an abundance of clean drinking water, which is rare in the Central Valleys of Oaxaca. But it becomes scarcer as the population increases.

In Zaachila, as in all of Oaxaca, people struggle to make ends meet. When I was a kid, we didn't have enough to eat and there weren't a lot of jobs available. I started working when I was six or eight, planting and weeding corn, collecting trash, sweeping the market, and helping my mom sell tortillas. These are the some of the experiences and conditions that shaped the way I see the world. It's different for kids who always got new shoes, who could go to college.

We're surrounded by lifestyles that don't have anything to do with our own interests, aspirations, hopes or dreams.

But why should we have to fight off someone always telling us what to think, to buy this brand of television or car? We can think and make decisions on our own. We're victims of the few economically-privileged who make decisions that end up affecting lots of people. We have the right to ask why. And from this why we can look for answers and initiate a process of transformation.

In Zaachila, there have always been people asking these questions. A few years ago, Coca-Cola wanted to build a plant here, which would supposedly bring lots of jobs to the community. But some people realized that they were going be using a tremendous amount of water, limiting what would be left for the rest of us. So a group of people organized and prevented the construction of the Coca-Cola plant. There have always been these activists; they just haven't been able to reach the majority of people in most cases. Authoritarian regimes always construct campaigns to discredit organizers, and try to convince people that protesters are crazy.

It wasn't until the severe repression, starting with the violent removal of the teachers' encampment on June 14th, that the majority of people started to see that there were fundamental problems here, and began to support the movement that has taken shape over the last year.

***

When the teachers' union was attacked, all the teachers in Zaachila starting organizing and brought people together. Early on in July, a month after the repression, people were called together by the ringing of the bells. The ringing of the bells in Zaachila is very symbolic, rooted in the tradition of blowing the conch shell. They're only rung under very special circumstances. In this case they were used to bring everyone to the city center for the first popular assembly. There we determined what the position of the town was in regards to our mayor, José Coronel Martínez, who had upset many people by sending the city police to back up the governor on June 14th. He also made people mad by organizing a number of so-called "Peace Marches" along with the PRI, paying people to march around town dressed in white to show their support for Governor Ulises.

So there were a series of meetings, where we discussed the movement and the role of our city government in the repression. We discovered things that we didn't expect that added to our more immediate frustrations. For example, we started to investigate and learned about a housing development deal that would strain the city water supply, but was approved because the developer had agreed to give eleven houses to the mayor and his friends. We also discovered a long history of misuse of funds intended for children, students, and the elderly. For the first time, the majority of the people in Zaachila started to see this corruption. So after ringing the bells and bringing people together, we decided that José Coronel needed to leave the municipal building and never come back.

However, just like Ulises Ruiz, he didn't accept the people's decision. He did leave the municipal building eventually, taking all the vehicles, computers, and files with him. But he took refuge in another community nearby and then started moving all around Oaxaca. He made the same declarations that Ulises Ruiz was making: "I'm not leaving" and "The people elected me" and "I don't listen to the APPO, only to my constituency."

Men, women, children, and city council members joined

together to take over the municipal building. A lot of the building was locked and we only used the hallways and the offices that were open. We stayed in the municipal building night and day, taking care of everything. And that's how the neighborhood assemblies were born. We'd say, "It's the neighborhood of La Soledad's turn and tomorrow it's up to San Jacinto." That's how the neighborhood assemblies were first used, and then later they turned into decision-making bodies, which is where we are now.

The seizing of the municipal building was totally spontaneous. The activists from before played a role and initially directed things, but the popular assembly structure was developed little by little, and many of the earlier activists dropped out of the movement because they had a different perspective of how social transformation would take place. Among the people most involved now, only a handful were activists before.

Taking over the municipal building brought the conflict in Oaxaca City here to Zaachila. We wanted José Coronel out of office as much as we wanted Ulises Ruiz out. We built barricades across the main roads in the city during the most intense moments of the conflict. We used the bells as a resource to alert people of confrontations between the APPO and police, so we could go and help those in Oaxaca City. When people heard the bells they came running with rocks, sticks, pistols, whatever they had available, ready to protect Zaachila from the state government. We had entered the struggle.

***

After seizing the municipal building, people interested in the transformation of Zaachila started to talk to each other.

Many different visions came to the forefront—some wanted to pave all the roads in the city, others wanted a hospital or a cultural institute. However, there were some of us that didn't look to the modern world for our transformation; we wanted to resurrect the forgotten structures of our ancestors. We began asking people how they wanted to see the city run; we looked into how things were organized in the past. Sure, there were people directing this initiative, but they would always ask the community, "Given the information we have, what do we do?" This process led to the creation of a permanent popular assembly to govern the city.

We didn't have a mayor, and we didn't want to submit to the authority of the state government, so we named our own people's mayor, and our own people's city council. Neighborhood assemblies, comprised of a rotating body of five people, were also formed in each section of town and together they would form the permanent popular assembly, the People's Council of Zaachila. The people from neighborhood assemblies may not be activists at all, but little by little, as they follow their obligation to bring information back and forth from the Council, they develop their capacity for leadership. All the agreements made in the Council are studied by these five people and then brought back to the neighborhoods for review. These assemblies are completely open; anyone can attend and have their voice heard. Decisions always go to a general vote, and all the adults present can vote. For example, if some people think a bridge needs to be built, and others think we need to focus on improving electricity, we vote on what the priority should be. The simple majority wins, fifty-percent plus one.

Once the Council was formed, it started to work with the scarce resources that were available. We got our funds from taxes on stands at the market. The economy of Zaachila didn't stop, and taxes on business are what maintained the Council. We named our own police force as well, composed of people from Zaachila and without any direct connection to the state government. Services began to be provided despite resource scarcity: trash pickup started, the water stayed on, public works continued.

People were very enthusiastic to begin with and responded to the needs of the new government. For example, on Christmas Eve we hold an important celebration in Zaachila and that first year, there weren't any city resources, but the people made it happen. They brought piñatas and all the food. It was an amazing experience. In the month of January, on Three Kings' Day, when all the kids were expecting toys, people brought tons of gifts to pass out to all the families. It was quite a surprise for everyone that with so little so much could be done. We realized that the strongest solidarity exists among those with very little. In fact, in some sense wealth has distanced us from our capacity, intrinsic to the human spirit, to build community.

***

From the heat of this movement the community radio station was born in Zaachila. But this doesn't mean that the groundwork hadn't been laid. For example, as the principal of an elementary school, I directed a kids' radio station, and one of my friends got me to bring the equipment to Oaxaca City to support the teacher's encampment. Later we saw the necessity of starting a community radio station in Zaachila, to share information about the movement, to coalesce divergent ideas and start to resolve conflicts. We asked the people's mayor if he would loan us space for the station in the municipal building. He brought the idea to the popular assembly and once they approved the idea, we brought all of my equipment to the building to get started. We began with the idea of providing a channel of communication for the movement, so that people could call in and communicate with each other. When there were meetings or mega-marches, we always broadcast the details on the radio.

But things didn't start out smoothly. We were always vulnerable to threats from paramilitaries and the state government. We operated under the assumption that someone might come to kill us or to take away all of the equipment. When we heard about threats, each of us would take part of the equipment and hide it somewhere, and then bring it back the next day. For a long time there was a warrant out for my arrest, and none of us could move around freely. For months the station was in limbo. Mostly youth were here keeping it alive. They were willing to stick around no matter what happened; they were dedicated to the station.

Little by little, we started to focus on what was going on here in the community of Zaachila. We invited people to share their experiences with us on air. We started to play the music that the people of Zaachila wanted to hear, rather than just streaming what was on *Radio Universidad* in Oaxaca City. When things calmed down, we started to expand our programming. We're lucky to have more than thirty people participating voluntarily who are all very professional. We have political talk shows, news shows, a poetry hour, alcoholics anonymous on the air, and a program where migrants come to share their experiences. We play protest music and we provide a variety of children's programming, which facilitates their self-expression. In our culture, adults are always the ones to answer the phone. When children call into the station and hear themselves on the radio it helps them build confidence to express themselves freely.

We want our radio to represent a symbol of resistance to the government and promote media that we ourselves create. We also want the radio to be a space where we generate new ideas. For example, the idea that we don't have to be capitalists, that we can make radio without paying salaries. And the idea that radio can be subversive, and bring us to new ways of organizing ourselves.

Through the radio, we have started to construct new identities, and because the people of Zaachila appreciate the work we do, they will protect us from the state government. While we've received threats, we haven't faced any direct government aggression because of our popular support.

***

Zaachila has already been an example for others. People start to ask, "Why does Zaachila have a community radio station and we don't?" Or: "Why does Zaachila have a popular assembly and we don't?" There's a lot of work to be done, but the seed has been sown.

Despite all the enthusiasm, in reality these are difficult times. There are elections in December for a new mayor, and we don't know what's going to happen. The People's Council of Zaachila has decided to support a candidate, and we've even given him airtime on the radio. This has been a challenge, because some think that it shouldn't be our role to get involved in the elections. If our candidate doesn't win, if the

PRI wins, we don't know what's going to happen to the radio or to Zaachila in general. But if we can maintain the neighborhood assembly structure, I don't think it matters who gets elected, we'll have our independence. These paths have not been traveled before, and we won't find answers in a book. Social movements can sometimes be short-sighted. We're looking for ways to move into the future. There are a lot of people ready to defend the system we've created.

Zaachila has survived so far because people are frustrated, not only with Ulises Ruiz or the former mayor, but with a whole political and economic system. It helped that there were people around to direct this frustration towards a certain end. In addition, the pride and identity of Zaachila has been strengthened by the people from all over the world that have come to recognize what we've done here. We've seen the links between the tanks of repression in Oaxaca and those in other countries. We recognize that we are part of an international movement. Eventually our struggles will unite; in this I'm almost positive. We may not be around to see it, but I think it has to be.

***

The diversity of cultures on this globe will make our struggles look different. We have to learn from all the different paths towards transformation, but if we try to come to some agreement, I don't think we'll ever be successful. Each of us has to do what we can in our communities. That's how broad transformation will take place.

In the struggle we find our reasons for living. There are those who want to live in a big house or have a nice car, and accept the happiness that's imposed on them by someone else. Maybe the work we do won't make us happy, but we're contributing to the transformation of reality and, at the same time, of ourselves.

The December 2007 election for Zaachila's mayor was won by the PRI by a narrow margin after a last minute split in the left. However, the radio continues to operate from another location. Several autonomous municipalities that formed during the popular movement remain in Oaxaca.

Conclusion

The Other Campaign, APPO and the Left: Reclaiming an Alternative

by Gustavo Esteva

I don't know how to say what I want to say. We're on the brink of a precipice, the sky's about to fall. At the same time, we're full of hope. We finally see the light at the end of the tunnel. How to explain this contradiction?

Words fail me. All the terms in which I was politically educated, especially those defining my political position and militancy up to now, seem increasingly inadequate in the world in which I live, to describe the present moment in Oaxaca, in Mexico, in the world…

I'm convinced that Zapatismo is today the most radical and perhaps most important political movement in the world, and that the Zapatistas' latest initiative, The Other Campaign, constitutes a real alternative in Mexico, perhaps the only one in the current political crisis. But that seems absurd. No one is paying attention to their proposals. The media, where all political activity seems to be concentrated, barely notes their existence. Is it true, as many think, that the Zapatistas missed their opportunity a long time ago, and march slowly but surely to their political extinction?

Background: The Political Transition in Mexico

In the year 2000, the Partido Revolucionario Institucional (PRI), the party which dominated the political structure of Mexico for 70 years, lost the presidential election. Let's not have illusions about what happened. An indigenous leader put it clearly: "For

331

us, the system is like a snake. Last night, it shed its skin. Now it's a different color, that's all." But we are fully aware of what we did: we got rid of the oldest authoritarian regime in the world.

Thus we catalyzed a political transition toward a new regime. But we're not yet there. What characterizes the current juncture is the struggle to define it and therefore also the nature of the transition. Some want to consolidate the regime that can be described as a neo-liberal republic. Others want to reorganize society from the bottom up and create an entirely different one.

We are suffering the impact of the North American Free Trade Agreement and all types of economic difficulties, social ills and political conflicts. Nonetheless, what defines our situation, what I smell at the grassroots, what feeds our hope, is the possibility that we're in the midst of the first social revolution of the 21st century, the revolution of the new commons. We are creating alternatives:

- We're organizing ourselves beyond "development," reclaiming our own definition of the good life.
- We're going beyond the economy. We, the so-called marginalized, are now marginalizing the economy in our lives.
- We're going beyond the individual in reclaiming our commons.
- We're moving beyond the nation-state in reclaiming a new political horizon.

We see globalization as an economic project that attempts to root homo economicus, the possessive individual of the West, throughout the planet under the hegemony of the United States and capital. This project has two attractive masks: a political mask, "democracy," and an ethical mask, "human rights." We are challenging three aspects of this project:

- We're resisting the trans-nationalized economy that encroaches upon and disrupts our lives
- We see their "democracy" as a structure of domination and control
- We perceive their "human rights" as the Trojan Horse of re-colonialization.

We don't accept globalization. For us it is neither promise nor reality; it is the emblem of a hegemonic project of domination.

End of the Old Regime

In December 1993, the dominant impression was that nothing could prevent Mexico from entering the First World. They had just accepted us in the club of rich countries. The World Bank touted Mexico as a model for everyone. I often heard, at that time, a comment in the middle and upper classes: "We're not going to live like the people in the United States, but better. We'll have all the goods and services they have…and in addition, servants." Obviously, this cynical observation didn't take into consideration the point of view of the servants. But that was the feeling. We were getting closer to the supposed paradise of the American Way of Life.

At that time, President Salinas was universally recognized as a leader who understood the way the wind was blowing and was pulling his country out of under-development. He was a candidate for the first director of the World Trade Organization, the institution quintessentially defining our times. He also commented that he didn't commit the error of Gorbachev: to start political reform before completing economic reform. He had used all the authoritarian instruments of the old regime to implement neoliberal economic reform, postponing the political. The opposition parties only offered variations of his model.

On January 1, 1994, a small group of Mayas, armed with machetes, sticks and a few guns, occupied four major cities of Chiapas and declared war on the Mexican government. It was the Zapatista Army of National Liberation (EZLN). A few days after the Zapatista uprising, there was an immense "aha!" effect. People could see that their problems were not personal, but rather social; we had an erroneous administration and a perverse president. As journalists began to go to the villages and file reports on the war, the media started showing the real Mexico. They began to show the Mexico of our dramas and misery, not that of new bridges and brilliant skyscrapers, which for years had created an illusion of a country that didn't exist— or existed for only a few. The people once again saw themselves in this dramatic reality. It was a revelation. The Zapatista slogan caught on immediately: "¡Basta ya!" ("Enough! Now I've had enough!")

The force that liquidated the old regime in Mexico thus crystallized, almost by surprise.

Construction of a New Regime

We're in transition from a conventional political power structure to an alternative form of social organization. In order to construct this alternative, we need to finish dismantling the old regime and reorganize society from the bottom up.

Our economy was a peculiar hybrid of capitalism. In 1982 the public sector represented 62% in a highly closed economy. The government controlled it completely. In 2000, due to the privatization frenzy, the public sector represented only 18% in one of the most open economies in the world. The Mexican economy had escaped from the control of the government... and of the country itself.

As regards political structure, with the mafia-like organization created by the PRI, which extended to the farthest reaches of the country, nothing moved without the will of the President. He had total control of his government: the executive branch, the judiciary branch, his political party, and through his party, of Congress. In those 70 years under the PRI, almost 500 amendments to the Constitution were introduced. All of them came from the President's initiative.

For 70 years, experts described our regime as a peculiar monarchy, which replaced the king every six years for another member of the so-called "revolutionary family", the group that inherited the power structure created by the 1910 revolution. This regime suffered a long-agonized end. A group of technocrats who took power in 1982 accelerated it. They used the authoritarian instruments of the old regime to dismantle it, to impose the neo-liberal catechism, procrastinating political reforms...until the Zapatista uprising. In the three weeks following, the regime was forced to make more concessions to the political opposition than in the previous 50 years.

At the beginning, the transition caused great disillusionment. Those who had fought against the old regime in the name of formal democracy were frustrated and depressed. Political campaigns, instead of providing opportunities for public debate and citizen participation, were reduced to a three-ring circus.

And instead of a popular government, capable of stopping the devastating neo-liberal tsunami, Vicente Fox, a wealthy businessman, ex-director of Coca Cola, became president and dedicated himself to consolidating that ideology.

While knowing that the nation-state is a structure of domination and control, a strait-jacket that restrains or prevents cultural diversity, the Zapatistas understood it as a provisional framework for the transition to a new form of social organization, with a different political horizon. What we're now doing in Mexico is to appeal to sociological and political imagination. As the Zapatistas say, to change the world is extremely difficult, if not impossible. But it is possible to create a new world. This is not a romantic dream, but a pragmatic attitude.

The Sixth Declaration of the Lacandon Jungle

On January 1, 2004, the Zapatistas used the celebration of their anniversary—the 10th of their uprising, the 20th of their creation—to redefine themselves. "20 years have thus elapsed," said Comandante Abraham. "But we're just beginning."

The report the Zapatistas presented in August 2004, on the operation of the *Juntas de Buen Gobierno,* confirmed their usual style: they say what they do and they do what they say. It also revealed the impressive progress they have achieved and the no less impressive obstacles they face. "The indigenous villages should organize and govern themselves according to their own ways of thinking and understanding, according to their interests, taking into account their cultures and traditions." (*La Jornada*, 10-08-04). Zapatismo, say the Zapatistas, is communities making their decisions against the grain of the dominant ideology.

Throughout 2006, Delegado Zero (Subcomandante Marcos) traveled throughout Mexico to organize The Other Campaign announced in the Sixth Declaration of the Lacandon Jungle, which includes an explicitly anti-capitalist orientation. The Other Campaign was very different from those organized by the presidential candidates for the July 2nd elections. While candidates were competing to be heard, delivering promises in order to get votes, The Other Campaign was creating conditions for people to listen to each other, find ways to articulate their discontent, and converge in a national program of struggle.

In the course of the year, one of the seeds planted by the Zapatistas started to bear fruit in Oaxaca, a state neighboring Chiapas—the only state in Mexico in which indigenous people constitute the majority and govern themselves, in their own way, in four-fifths of the municipalities of the state.

The Oaxacan Riddle

The Popular Assembly of the Peoples of Oaxaca (APPO) has had immense visibility but it continues to be a mystery. What kind of organization is this? What is the nature of this peculiar political animal? Is it a revolt? A rebellion? A popular insurrection? Is it the beginning of a social revolution or merely an explosion against a despotic governor?

On June 14th, Oaxaca's governor, Ulises Ruiz, brutally repressed a sit-in organized by the local teachers' union to demand its annual salary claims. The repression sparked a movement, which quickly articulated the immense discontent in the state. What looked like a mere revolt—a popular explosion against a tyrannical governor and was later perceived as a rebellion against the authoritarianism of the regime—clearly manifested itself as a social and political movement of a new breed, of great social and historical depth and scope.

The APPO is the product of a slow accumulation of forces and many lessons gathered during previous struggles. The APPO became in very short time the main player in the political life of Oaxaca, and coalesced organizationally in assembly style, without leaders or formal structures. Born at the grassroots, from the core of Oaxacan society, the movement expressed a profound discontent, which found in Ulises Ruiz an apt emblem of everything that they wanted to change.

The APPO has creatively applied the policy of one NO and many YESes, with people united in a common rejection, for various motives, reasons and ideals, but also acknowledging the plurality of society with an attitude of inclusiveness.

The main challenge is to put the struggle to improve formal democracy and participatory democracy (popular initiatives, referendums, plebiscites, the right to recall elected leaders, participatory budgeting, etc.) at the service of the struggle for radical democracy—extending to the whole state the indigenous communities' tradition of self-governance. Oaxacans are not waiting for the inevitable departure of Ulises Ruiz to put ideas into action; there are already many APPOs operating around the state on community, neighborhood, municipal and regional levels.

In Oaxaca, the fraudulently constituted powers no longer function. From July to November, there were no police in the city of Oaxaca, and all public offices were closed by the APPO, which established permanent sit-ins in front of every one of them. The displaced officials had to meet secretly in hotels or private homes. The police could leave their quarters only at night, surreptitiously, to launch guerilla attacks against the people. The APPO showed amazing capacities for autonomous self-government. There were fewer crimes and assaults in those six months than in any other similar period during the last ten years.

The APPO wisely refrained from attempting to seize power and kept itself as close as possible to the political traditions of Oaxaca's indigenous communities. Rather than climbing into the empty chairs of those who abused power, APPO has been strengthening social networks and reinforcing the dignity and autonomy of Oaxacans. Proclamations of APPO's good government decrees represent an appeal to free men and women who, with extraordinary courage, a healthy dose of common sense, and surprising ingenuity, are attempting to rebuild society from the bottom up and create a new set of social relations beyond capitalism. As the Zapatistas advised, rather than trying to change the world, Oaxacans today are more pragmatically trying to construct a new one.

On October 27, 2006 paramilitaries and municipal policemen loyal to Ulises Ruiz attacked the barricades that the APPO set up throughout the center of Oaxaca. In one of these, they shot and killed Brad Will, an American journalist with deep sympathies for the peoples of Oaxaca. Violent confrontations broke out around the city. That evening President Fox used the murder as an excuse to send in the federal police.

The APPO explicitly decided to resist non-violently, avoiding confrontation. In the face of the federal police, with its tanks and all the paraphernalia of power, the people of Oaxaca exhibited enormous restraint. Unarmed citizens stopped tanks by laying their bodies on the pavement. Women offered flowers to the police. When police occupied the main plaza of Oaxaca City, the APPO abandoned it and regrouped on the university campus, protecting their radio station, which transmitted the decision to remain non-violent and avoid confrontation and provocation. Outside the university, meanwhile, police began to selectively arrest APPO members at the barricades. By the end of the day, there were three dead, many injured, and many more disappeared. Those picked up by the police were sequestered in military barracks.

Human rights organizations, including the government's own National Commission on Human Rights, were unable to visit or even identify those who had been arrested because the police moved them secretly from one place to another. In the following days, people coming from surrounding villages to support the movement were pulled out of trucks, beaten, and arrested. In the occupied city, the police committed all kinds of abuses, while Ulises Ruiz's thugs and hit-men went about their business with impunity.

The battle of November 2, 2006, when the people resisted an attack on the university by the federal police, was the largest and most violent clash between civilians and police in Mexico's history, and perhaps the only one that resulted in an unquestionable popular triumph. The fight was certainly unequal enough. Although the police were outnumbered five or six to one, if we count children, they had shields and other weapons, not to mention tanks and helicopters, while the people had only sticks, stones, a few slingshots, and some uninvited Molotov cocktails.

On November 25, 2006 the APPO fell into a trap organized by the federal police, which used provocateurs and similar strategies. At the end of a peaceful APPO march, a very violent repression started. Two international commissions visiting Oaxaca gave national and international visibility to the horror: at least 17 killed, many disappeared and injured, more than 500 jailed, and all kinds of serious violations of human rights, including sexual abuse of men and women. By mid-December, most of the federal police had left the state. Local police have been patrolling the city since then and "guarding" strategic points.

But the movement continues. Brutal repression inhibited the movement as it sought its natural course but did not stop it. Upstream, uncontainable forces gain strength. The challenge is to find their natural course in time to avoid a devastating flood. This is also, perhaps, the present situation of the country.

Felipe Calderón took office as Mexico's President in the midst of an open social and political confrontation. In his administration, the State's crisis of legitimacy will deepen, as will social polarization and economic difficulties, along with acceleration of the destruction of the environment, violence in all spheres, and social decomposition. He will use repression or open militarization against growing popular discontent.

In Oaxaca, the entire political apparatus supports a disreputable governor, and spectacularly demonstrates that it uses its monopoly on violence to attack the people and protect those in power. But he who sows violence, reaps it in kind. That's where we are.

Subcomandante Marcos declared that Calderón "is going to start to fall from his first day in office" and that "we're on the eve of a great uprising or civil war." When asked who would lead that uprising, he replied, "the people, each in their place, in a network of mutual support. If we don't accomplish it that way, there will be spontaneous uprisings, explosions all over, civil war…"

He cited the case of Oaxaca, where "there are no leaders,

nor bosses: it's the people themselves who are organized." That's how it is going to be in the whole country; Oaxaca is a bell weather of what's going to happen all over. "If there isn't a civil and peaceful way out, which is what we propose in the Other Campaign," Marcos warned, "then it will become each man for himself...For us, it doesn't matter what's above. What matters is what's going to arise from below. When we rise up, we're going to sweep away the entire political class, including those who say they're the parliamentary left."

This is a clear depiction of the challenges that lie ahead. The Other Campaign and the Zapatistas, like APPO, find themselves exposed to a two-pronged attack: the constituted powers with their paramilitary groups that systematically threaten them and the institutional left that tries to isolate, marginalize and discredit them. It will be difficult, in such circumstances, to achieve the articulation of "pockets of resistance" that exist throughout the country into the "network of mutual support" that Zapatistas have been trying to create. No one can say whether the Zapatistas will be able to unify all the discontented into broad coalitions that could put into practice a "national program of struggle" in a great civil, democratic and peaceful uprising. But the alternative couldn't be worse: a government ruling by force and with the market; the reign of drug dealers spreading and deepening; increasingly violent forms of civil war, exploding throughout the country, in which people confront the constituted powers, local mafias, paramilitary groups and their own demons.

Far from being anomalous, this looks like the current state of affairs in many parts of the world—as people coming from more than 40 countries discussed in the Zapatista meeting in Oventic, on January 1, 2007. In spite of dark prospects, the debates were a clear source of hope. Nonconformity and discontent are not enough. Neither is critical awareness. People mobilize themselves when they think their action may bring about a change, when they have hope. And that is what more and more people have today.

This text, translated and edited by Holly Yasui, is a synthesis of a talk given in the Center for Global Justice conference "Another World is Necessary" in San Miguel de Allende, July 2007, using excerpts from the book Celebration of Zapatismo (Mexico, Ediciones ¡Basta!, 2005). The complete version of the talk can be seen in Znet.

Teaching Rebellion Study Guide

What can we learn from this movement?
by Patrick Lincoln

As the social movement in Oaxaca responded to repression and grew, as the APPO developed, as radio and television stations were taken over, and as people continued their struggle in the face of assassinations and harassment, activists, organizers, independent journalists, and curious onlookers came from all around Mexico and the world looking for lessons. As one Oaxacan organizer put it, "because they thought nothing like this could happen where they lived."

The solidarity work that C.A.S.A. has engaged in over this last year has raised questions about our role and influence as foreigners in a movement rooted in a particular identity, place and history. We recognize the tendency to romanticize the struggles of others before thinking critically about strategies to deepen our own communities of resistance.

These testimonies give the reader a personal and complex picture of Oaxacan organizing. While lived in similar ways by many movement activists, each story is a unique experience, firmly located in the heart, mind and spirit of the individual teller, with its own truth to share. The following exercises— which reference the testimonies, the chronology of the popular uprising and the historic context— are designed to push us past the passive role of reading about what happened somewhere else and towards the active role of thinking critically about ways we can make change happen in our own communities.

This study guide will be the most useful for a discussion group that will meet on more than one occasion. However, modify the exercises as necessary.

Individual Reflection

These questions are designed to be considered individually, with the highlighted testimonies as an inspiration. It will be helpful to give sufficient time, even a few days, to come up with responses. Each person should create a way to present their responses to the group—for example, a drawing, list, or short essay.

1. From the testimonies of Eleuterio and Marinita, it's apparent that state repression of the teacher's encampment encouraged a broad-based response in solidarity. What were the different factors that pulled people out into the streets? What motivations would get ordinary people active in your community?

2. Genoveva and Aurelia also discuss the influence of repression on their formation as social activists. How do you think you or your community might respond to similar situations? Think of three things that allow someone to experience such difficulty and move forward in struggle rather than to lose all hope?

3. Marcos and Ekaterine mention the indigenous culture and organization that contributed to building a movement that went beyond reacting to a repressive government and towards creating alternatives. What exists in the culture of your community that can inspire a movement for something new? What traditional stories or practices shed light on how your struggles will look?

4. Derwin recounts how his father and whole family have influenced his developing perception of the world, and his role in making a difference. What childhood experiences have most shaped your view of the world? Who did/do you look to as an example of how to act in this world?

PAIR STUDY

Find a partner for the following activities. It's not important that the entire book be read by both of you, but it may be useful to start by sharing experiences and information on the chosen theme.

For each theme, two testimonies are listed. Both people choose one to read, then consider the questions individually. After 20-30 minutes, come back together as pairs to share responses, referencing pieces of the testimony that made a particularly strong impression on your answers.

Media—Tonia and Adán.

1. Identify the different roles played by the media during the movement in Oaxaca 2006.

2. Explain how you would define community-controlled media as different from commercial, and even independent, media.

3. How is commercial media used in your community, and what can activists learn from Oaxaca about the use of information?

Neighborhood Organizing—Silvia and David

1. List the different roles the barricades played in the movement in Oaxaca.

2. Describe the area that surrounds where you are currently living. What assumptions do you have about your neighbors, and what assumptions do you think they have about you?

3. What permanent structures could be created to bring people together in your communities?

External Solidarity—Gustavo and Jenny

1. What were the specific characteristics of the movement that attracted support from those outside of Oaxaca?

2. How do you think international activists could have, or did, affect the movement?

3. What does solidarity mean to you, especially as someone on the outside of a particular struggle?

Party Politics—Carlos and David

1. According to what you've read, describe the interaction between social movements and political parties in Mexico. Why might some choose to support a candidate and others reject voting altogether?

2. How might social movements use political parties as tools

for change, and how might governments use them as tools for repression or cooptation?

3. What tensions exist in your communities around electoral politics—for example, whether or not to support a certain candidate, to vote, or to meet with elected city officials? How do you see these tensions affect organizing?

GROUP ACTIVITIES

The following activities are designed for large and small groups. If there are more than 15 people present for the large group exercises, break into groups of 4 or 5 for small group discussion, with a report-back to the whole group afterwards. It will be helpful, but not necessary, if everyone has read a good portion of the book or at least has some working knowledge of the movement in Oaxaca. The three activities may work best if done together, in the following order.

The Influence of History (60-90 min)

Read one of the testimonies out loud as a large group (Carmelina, Carlos, or David might work well).

Read the Historic Context in small groups, with individuals to read quietly to themselves first, highlighting passages that stand out for them. After 5-10 minutes, small groups discuss what each person highlighted, and the role of history in shaping our current struggles. The large group comes back together to list a few responses from each small group.

As a large group, the following questions could be useful for a concluding discussion:

1. What do you think is missing from the Historic Context? What questions are you left with?

2. How does the historic relationship between the Mexican government and social movements compare to the history of your country?

3. What lessons can be taken from our collective histories? (Be as concrete as possible)

Chronology of the Popular Uprising (30-45 min)

Recreate the chronology of the popular uprising ("Pillars of the State" and "Pillars of the People") on butcher paper and tape it to a wall for everyone to see. Hand out post-it notes to everyone in the room. Read the chronology events out loud. Invite everyone to place post-it notes directly onto the chronology over events that stand out to them, with a few phrases explaining why they may be similar to experiences they've had, or why they may seem particularly significant, etc. Some call these "Aha!" moments.

After everyone has placed their post-it notes, read them out loud and ask their authors to explain why they chose to place the post-it note there.

Pillars of the State and Pillars of the People: Repression and Resistance (60-90 min)

It's often said that repression is built upon a series of pillars, and that our role as social movements is to push those pillars back, giving us more space to create alternatives, and to remove them entirely when and where we can.

Our social movements are built on pillars as well—our visions for new worlds, the strategies we use to guide us, and the tactics that make our work concrete every day. The following activity is designed to help identify the pillars of the state and of the people within the movement in Oaxaca, 2006, but most importantly, to help us identify the pillars of repression and resistance in our own communities.

Through this process of comparison and self-awareness, the hope is that our struggles will become more effective, and that avenues for the construction of new pillars of resistance will be discovered. For example, a pillar of resistance may be holding a community meeting where common problems are defined and working groups are formed to create strategies for addressing those problems. However, a pillar of repression may then be the financing of an electoral campaign, which incorporates a platform based on the community-defined problems but none of the strategies developed. How do we move forward, and refine our work in this context?

On a piece of butcher paper, draw 4 or 5 pillars of repression towards the top of the paper, and below 4 or 5 pillars of resistance. On another piece of butcher paper, draw another complete set of pillars.

Break into groups of 2 or 3. Hand out 12 post-it notes or small pieces of paper to each group. Invite each group to think of 3 strategies or tactics of government repression that were used in Oaxaca, and 3 strategies or tactics of movement resistance. After 10-15 minutes, one person from the first group places her post-it notes on the butcher paper, one post-it note per pillar, for both repression and resistance.

As the remaining groups have their turn, they each have

the chance to place their post-it notes on the same pillars as earlier groups if they see a connection, or to create a new pillar if what they've written is identified as a separate strategy or tactic.

After all of the post-its have been placed for each group, read each one out loud to discuss if any need to be moved, if new pillars should be created, and how each pillar could be labeled if there is one way to encompass all of the strategies or tactics written below.

Repeat the same process, but this time using the strategies and tactics of your group's home government, and the movements you either have experience in, or are familiar with. If the group is too diverse for one location to work, ask each individual to contribute based on her own experiences.

After the creation of both sets of pillars, use the following questions as guides to conclude:

1. What differences exist between the repression and resistance in Oaxaca and what you have experience with?

2. What similarities and connections are there between the two sets of pillars?

3. What of our pillars of resistance might be ineffective entirely in the face of state repression and need to be replaced?

4. In what ways can we strengthen our pillars of resistance and give more space for our movements to grow?

CHRONOLOGY OF THE POPULAR UPRISING

PILLARS of the STATE

JUNE 14, 2006

At 4:30 am police attempt to displace the teachers' plantón in the city center, using tear gas, firearms and helicopters in the attack. Thousands of people from around the city come to the teachers' aid and after 5 hours of confrontation, the zócalo is retaken from the police. The union's radio station and voice of the movement, Radio Plantón, is targeted. Police brutalize station operators and destroy the broadcasting equipment. The movement's radio transmission continues from Radio Universidad at the Benito Juárez Autonomous University of Oaxaca (UABJO) until the end of November.

PILLARS of the PEOPLE

MAY 22, 2006

Teachers from the historically active Section XXII of the national teachers' union officially initiate a strike and a plantón, occupying 50 blocks in the city's center to demand more resources for education and better working conditions.

JUNE 2, 2006

The First Megamarch is convened when the government fails to act in response to the teachers' demands; thousands take to the streets to demand a trial for repressive state governor Ulises Ruiz Ortiz.

JUNE 7, 2006

Between 120,000 and 200,000 people participate in the Second Megamarch. Various social and neighborhood organizations, unions and communities that have survived government repression hold a popular trial for Ulises Ruiz.

JUNE 15, 2006

Though a curfew was imposed in the city the previous night, teachers from Section XXII return to the plantón with the support of the healthcare workers' union and students.

JUNE 16, 2006

Around 500,000 people participate in the Third Megamarch,

demanding federal intervention to remove Governor Ulises Ruiz from office as well as to call attention to a wide array of social and political grievances.

JUNE 17-18, 2006

The Popular Assembly of the Peoples of Oaxaca (APPO by its Spanish initials) is formed, and soon grows to include more than 300 unions, social organizations, indigenous communities, collectives, neighborhoods and student groups.

JUNE 28, 2006

More than 500,000 attend the Fourth Megamarch, demanding the resignation of Ulises Ruiz, an end to the repression and freedom for all political prisoners.

JULY 17, 2006

The APPO reaffirms its boycott of the state-sponsored commercial Guelaguetza festival, and the event is cancelled at the last minute by the government "in order to avoid confrontations."

JULY 24, 2006

More than 20,000 attend the APPO sponsored People's Guelaguetza, a vibrant event with presentations of traditional dances and music from the 7 regions of the state.

JULY 26, 2006

In a day of coordinated protests, later known as the "July 26"

JUNE 22, 2006

Ulises Ruiz convenes a march of support for the government, bribing and blackmailing people to participate. Such blatant corruption is denounced, many calling it the "March of Shame". This tension produces confrontations in several parts of the city.

JULY 2, 2006

Presidential elections are held in Mexico. Conservative PAN candidate Felipe Calderón wins by a slim margin over center-left PRD candidate Andrés Manuel López Obrador, amidst numerous reports of irregularities. In state elections in Oaxaca, the PRI loses the majority of state districts for the first time in history.

JULY 22, 2006

The studios of the movement's new voice, Radio Universidad, are shot at with bullets by armed unknowns.

AUGUST 8, 2006

In another day of confrontations, Marcos García Tapia, professor of dentistry at UABJO, is gunned down in the city's historic center.

AUGUST 9, 2006

In the Putla region of the state, members of the community organization MULTI (Independent Triqui Movement for Unification and Struggle) are ambushed by gunmen and

PILLARS of the STATE

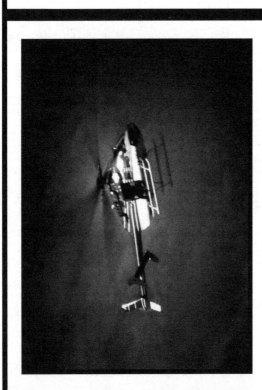

three of the group's members are killed including 35 year-old Andrés Santiago Cruz, 70 year-old Pedro Martínez Martínez and 11 year-old Pablo Octavio Martínez Martínez.

AUGUST 10, 2006
Snipers attack a peaceful march convened by the teachers' union, killing mechanic José Jimenez Colmenares as he accompanies his wife, a member of the teachers union.

PILLARS of the PEOPLE

Offensive," teachers from the union and the APPO block highways to Veracruz and Guerrero and occupy numerous government buildings including the Supreme Court, the Attorney General's office and the Capitol. Representatives of the APPO travel to Mexico City to present a petition to the Senate demanding the resignation of Ulises Ruiz.

JULY 31, 2006
A popular government, based on assembly, is installed in Zaachila after the movement takes over the municipal government and establishes a community radio.

AUGUST 1, 2006
Thousands of women take to the streets in the March of Pots and Pans. After demonstrations in the city center, the women decide to march to Channel 9, the state-run radio and TV station. They peacefully occupy the building and begin to broadcast, transforming the state-controlled broadcasting into community-run media.

AUGUST 17-18, 2006
Hundreds participate in "Constructing Democratic Government in Oaxaca," one of many forums held to incorporate community proposals and initiatives.

AUGUST 20, 2006
In the early morning hours, the occupied Channel 9 is attacked

AUGUST 16, 2006
Retired teacher Gonzalo Cisneros Gautier is assassinated in Zaachila.

AUGUST 22, 2006
Public official and APPO sympathizer, Lorenzo San Pablo Cervantes is assassinated by state police forces near La Ley radio station.

SEPTEMBER 18, 2006 The PRI produced documents requesting the intervention of national security forces from the government. The teachers' union agrees to return to classes immediately if Ulises Ruiz would resign.

by paramilitary and police forces who destroy the broadcasting equipment and violently displace the media activists. The APPO and the teachers' union respond by taking over all 12 commercial radio stations in Oaxaca by dawn. All but two of the stations are returned to their owners later that day.

AUGUST 21, 2006
Community members respond to a call to construct barricades throughout the city to protect radio stations and impede the passage of the paramilitary and police forces patrolling the city. Up to 1,000 barricades are constructed every night until the final one is dismantled at the end of November.

PILLARS of the STATE

SEPTEMBER 30, 2006

Oaxaca becomes increasingly militarized as Army and Navy helicopters circle the capital city. 30 military trucks are deployed in the isthmus and reinforcement troops arrive by sea in Huatulco. This military presence makes the possibility of negotiation between the APPO and the government still more unlikely.

OCTOBER 2, 2006

Police open fire on the topiles in San Antonio de Castillo Velasco with AK-47's, killing Arcadio Fabián Hernández Santiago.

OCTOBER 3, 2006

PILLARS of the PEOPLE

SEPTEMBER 16, 2006

The traditional military parade to celebrate Mexico's Independence Day is replaced by four separate marches led by the APPO. José Cruz Luna, an indigenous Zapotec, reenacts Miguel Hidalgo's original Call for Independence, which is customarily a duty of heads of state.

SEPTEMBER 17, 2006

A sudden surge of popular assembly governments are seen in the regions of the Mixteca, Mazateca, Sierra Norte, Istmo, Mixe and Triqui as well as Mexico City and the states of Michoacán and Guerrero, and Baja California.

SEPTEMBER 21, 2006

The March for the Dignity of the Oaxacan People departs from Oaxaca for Mexico City.

OCTOBER 9, 2006

After 540 kilometers and 21 days, The March for the Dignity of the Oaxacan People arrives in Mexico City and creates a plantón in front of the Senate.

OCTOBER 14, 2006

The APPO begins a 28 day hunger strike in Mexico City.

OCTOBER 25, 2006

More than 200 civic organizations, the APPO, and representatives

While marching from Oaxaca to Mexico City, José Manuel Castro Patiño, a professor and member of the Ixtlán section of the teachers' union, dies from cardiac arrest as the march passes Amilcingo.

OCTOBER 14, 2006

APPO militant Alejandro García Hernández is assassinated by a soldier.

OCTOBER 18, 2006

Gunmen attack members of the APPO returning from an assembly, killing teacher and APPO leader Pánfilo Hernández.

OCTOBER 27, 2006

A statewide strike begins in the morning and the barricades are installed early in the day. A wave of violent and coordinated attacks are unleashed against the movement, and armed confrontation at barricades lead to the murders of at least 5 members of the movement: Emilio Alonso Fabián and Esteban López Zurita in Santa María Coyotepec; Esteban Ruíz and Bradley Roland Will in Santa Lucía del Camino; and Eudecacia Olivero Díaz en route to the hospital. The federal government uses these attacks as a pretext to send in Federal Police to Oaxaca, despite previous claims that the troops would not be sent.

OCTOBER 28, 2006

The federal government gives the APPO an ultimatum: "hand

from indigenous communities hold an assembly called "Citizens' Initiative for Dialogue towards Peace, Democracy and Justice in Oaxaca" to construct a new social pact with the aim of installing governance, rule of law, concern for human rights and a new constitutional order with authentic representation of the people of Oaxaca.

OCTOBER 30, 2006

Displaced from the city center by federal forces, the APPO opens a new plantón in front of the Santo Domingo cathedral. Thousands march in Oaxaca. The Zapatista Army of National Liberation erects roadblocks in Chiapas, and demonstrations

over Oaxaca or we will take it." Thousands of troops from the Army, Navy and the Federal Preventive Police are deployed.

OCTOBER 29, 2006

Confrontations erupt throughout the city in resistance to the arrival of the Federal Preventative Police. The violence results in three more slain activists; José Alberto López Bernal dies from the impact of a tear gas canister; Fidel Sánchez García is stabbed by a group of masked men and Roberto López Hernández falls in a confrontation at the Brenamiel barricade.

OCTOBER 31, 2006

Federal Police begin to take down barricades in the city, and their presence reinforces the intelligence and coordination of paramilitary groups carrying out attacks on the movement.

NOVEMBER 20, 2006

Around 2,000 demonstrators from the teachers' union and the APPO march to celebrate 106 years of resistance in Mexico. A confrontation breaks out and, during 4 hours, police launch tear gas and marble bullets at protestors who defend themselves with rocks. More than 53 protestors are reported injured and many more are detained and tortured.

NOVEMBER 25, 2006

Hundreds of thousands attend the Seventh Megamarch to

and direct actions take place in many cities, throughout México and internationally.

NOVEMBER 2, 2006

In an attempt to destroy the barricade that protected state university UABJO and Radio Universidad studios, federal forces attack from land and air. People from all over the city respond to calls for reinforcement and eventually overwhelm the PFP;

who return to their encampment in the zócalo without successfully destroying the barricade. The 7-hour confrontation leaves 200 activists and 10 police injured.

NOVEMBER 13, 2006
The APPO's state congress opens its first session with 260 representatives from all over the state.

NOVEMBER 19, 2006
Hundreds of women lead a march from the plantón in response to sexual violence against women at the hands of federal police.

NOVEMBER 29, 2006
At the end of the Forum of the Indigenous Peoples of Oaxaca,

demand the departure of Ulises Ruiz and the Federal Police. Protestors encircle the PFP in order to hold a vigil in the city center for 48 hours. Fierce police repression leaves more than 140 injured and hundreds arrested, disappeared and tortured. Numerous buildings are destroyed by fire—purportedly set by infiltrators as a pretext for the repression.

NOVEMBER 26, 2006
Protected by heavily armed police and helicopters, Ulises Ruiz

PILLARS of the STATE

holds a press conference in Santo Domingo to denounce the damages supposedly caused by protestors. Federal police raid houses in which APPO leaders are thought to be hiding; arbitrary detentions continue over the following days.

DECEMBER 3, 2006

Shortly after the announcement that negotiations would reopen between the APPO and the federal government, Marcelino Coache Verano, Ignacio Garcia Maldonado, Flavio and Horacio Sosa Villavicencio are arrested on their way to the negotiation table.

APRIL 13, 2007

David Venegas Reyes, APPO representative and member of VOCAL (Oaxacan Voices Constructing Autonomy and Liberty), is detained by plainclothes officers who plant drugs on his person as a pretext for his arrest.

JUNE 14, 2007

Thousands march to commemorate the one-year anniversary of the violent attempt to displace the teachers' plantón, and the subsequent formation of the APPO. Numerous aggressions are reported, including an attack against recently released former APPO spokeperson Marcelino Coache.

PILLARS of the PEOPLE

14 groups sign a resolution condemning the presence of the Federal Police in Oaxaca.

MARCH 17, 2007

The Peoples of the Isthmus in Defense of the Earth and in Resistance to Plan Puebla Panamá is created in La Venta, one of the communities most affected by neo-liberal development in the isthmus. Community leaders from La Venta, La Ventosa, La Mata, San Dionisio, Santo Domingo, members of the APPO and UCIZONI come together to organize a united front against the massive windmill construction project displacing people from their lan

JULY 14, 2007

In preparation for the second annual People's Guelaguetza, state and federal police, together with the military, construct roadblocks leading to the Guelaguetza stadium to prevent the event from being held. The APPO declares a red alert and announces that the Guelaguetza will be held in the Plaza de la Danza.

JULY 16, 2007

Thousands march to celebrate the People's Guelaguetza when violence breaks out at the military and police blockade the Guelaguetza stadium. More than 60 are arrested and at least 50 are injured. Emeterio Marino Cruz is nearly killed and suffers permanent brain damage from the impact of a tear gas canister.

Historic Context

This overview of the last 500 years of Mexican history is provided to contextualize the uprising in Oaxaca for readers less familiar with key events that have shaped the modern political and social climate in the country. A particular emphasis is placed on more recent events in order to understand that the explosive climate that prevails in Oaxaca is not isolated, but generalized throughout the country.

COLONIZATION

• By the end of the 15th century, prior to European colonization, an estimated 25 million native people live in North America alone (now 1.5 million). In the territories now known as Mexico, this includes the large and developed Aztec military empire, various communalistic societies of hunter-gatherers, the Zapotec and Mixtec civilizations of Oaxaca and many others.

• Columbus sets sail from Spain in 1492, supposedly in search of a new trade route to the West Indies, when he "discovers" America—opening up the western hemisphere for European colonization.

• Through wars of extermination and Christian evangelization, Spanish conquistadores attempt to subjugate and assimilate indigenous people throughout Mexico and Mesoamerica. The land, natural resources, forced or slave labor and precious metals extracted from "New Spain" serve as the basis for the power and influence of the Spanish throne in the early stages of capitalism.

- In the first hundred years of colonization, indigenous populations are decimated by disease, exploitation, and massacres carried out to secure Spain's political and ideological domination in the region.

- Spain and other European countries become dominant world powers as a direct result of their exploitation of the land, natural resources and human labor in Africa and the Americas. This legacy continues today with the economic, political and cultural dominance of white Europeans and their descendents.

- Oaxaca, the state with the largest indigenous population in Mexico—including 16 distinct ethnic groups and 26 distinct languages—retains diverse customs and systems of governance of these peoples. The numerous community assemblies and traditional decision-making bodies have been grouped under the term "usos y costumbres."

INDEPENDENCE

- The Mexican War of Independence (1810-1821) begins as a peasants' rebellion against colonial masters.

- Drawing from centuries of native resistance to colonial rule, Miguel Hidalgo, a criollo priest of a small town in Guanajuato, becomes chief instigator of the Mexican Independence Movement in 1810. During church discussion groups held in his home, he begins promoting the idea of an uprising by native and mixed-blood peasantry against the wealthy Spanish elite.

- Hidalgo is put to death in 1811 after an unsuccessful attempt to take Mexico City with his army.

- The scattered guerrilla forces from the Independence Movement gain momentum after Mexican elites join the struggle as a liberal regime temporarily takes power in Spain.

- Agustín de Iturbide, who had once persecuted Hidalgo's army, becomes the leader of this new struggle. Although he aligns himself with the opposition, he is ultimately committed to the defense of property rights and the social privileges of the elite criollo class.

- Independence doesn't translate into social transformation. White criollos like Iturbide ascend to the top of the social ladder while indigenous people and mestizos continued to occupy the lower ranks. The Roman Catholic Church retains its influence and religious monopoly.

REVOLUTION

- In 1857 Benito Juárez, Oaxaca native and Mexico's president, issues a new constitution inspired by that of the United States in an effort to abolish the remaining colonial structures. Civil war breaks out between the liberal, led by Juárez, and the conservatives, aligned with the entrenched Catholic hierarchy. Juárez is victorious and some of his reforms help lessen the excessive power of the church and the army.

- In 1876 another Oaxacan, Porfirio Díaz, becomes president and pushes through constitutional reforms that allow him to remain in office for thirty years. His model of industrial expansion—which translates to a combination of foreign direct investment and repressive political domination—is a factor in creating the conditions that fuel the revolution beginning in 1910.

• Oaxacan anarchist and founding member of the Mexican Liberal Party, Ricardo Flores Magón, is one of the more visible activists who organizes discontent against the Díaz regime, participating in and promoting social revolt more than a decade before the Revolution is initiated.

• The 1910 revolt is declared by Francisco Madero from exile in the United States, but aims primarily at the overthrow of Díaz without advocating substantive change. With conservative support, another general, Victoriano Huerta, overthrows Madero, who is, in turn, overthrown by rich landowner Venustiano Carranza.

• Behind the elite power struggle for the presidency, mestizo and indigenous peasants continue the revolt, heavily influenced by an earlier movement led by the Oaxacan anarchist Ricardo Flores Magón and his Mexican Liberal Party.

• With the support from the peasantry, Pancho Villa and Emiliano Zapata become the two key figures in the struggle against Huerta and Carranza. Villa is based in the north and builds a broad movement focused on the nationalization of industry and the expansion of the middle-class. Zapata, more influenced by Magón and indigenous communalism, is based in the southern state of Morelos and organizes campesino forces around the demand for the socialization of land encompassed in his famous cry: "Tierra y Libertad," –Land and Freedom.

• By 1920, and with support from the United States, England, France and Germany, the popular uprising is crushed. Some of the land-redistribution that Zapata demanded is incorporated in Carranza's 1917 Constitution, and briefly enacted under the administration of Lázaro Cárdenas in the 1930's, but these reforms never reach many parts of the country.

• A new political party, the PNR (now the PRI), consolidates power, reverses land reforms and contributes to an increasing rich/poor divide after the depression of the 1930's.

• Mexico's federal government operates under a single-party system until 2000 when Vicente Fox, of the right-wing opposition party, PAN, is elected president.

• In Oaxaca, however, the PRI has maintained its control over state politics for almost eighty years, and many consider the Mexican Revolution to be a process that continues.

TLATELOLCO STUDENT MASSACRE

• During most of 1968, student organizing in Mexico City focuses on government repression of the growing student and social movements. Seeking to paint a picture of stability prior to the opening of the Olympics in Mexico, these movements are declared to be part of a communist conspiracy, and government repression increases.

• As a broad range of workers become involved in the movement, the prospect of truly democratic change in Mexican society becomes more real.

• On the night of October 2, 1968, a meeting in the Plaza de las Tres Culturas is scheduled between the students and representatives of the Mexican government to start a process aimed at resolving the crisis. Instead, 300 to 500 students and workers are brutally murdered by government forces, and in the following week thousands are arrested and disappeared.

• The massacre continues to be commemorated every October 2nd, and the student movement set a precedent for large demonstrations in Mexico.

THE NORTH AMERICAN
FREE TRADE AGREEMENT (NAFTA)

• In response to economic crises in Mexico provoked by international markets, neo-liberal economic reforms are implemented from the beginning of the 1980s. The anti-popular nature of these reforms becomes quickly evident, and the PRI resorts to massive electoral fraud to steal the 1988 presidential elections from popular opposition candidate Cuauhtémoc Cardenas. Carlos Salinas de Gortari remains president in spite of the fraud, and paves the way for NAFTA by dismantling Article 27 of the Constitution, ending a historic promise for land reform.

• In 1994, NAFTA is signed into law by the governments of the United States, Canada and Mexico. It provides incentives for the United States to dump excess agricultural and manufactured goods in Mexico and refocuses the Mexican economy on the export of products made with cheap labor. The total abandonment of Mexico's domestic agricultural sector has had disastrous consequences for Mexico's majority campesino class.

THE ZAPATISTA ARMY
OF NATIONAL LIBERATION (EZLN)

• On January 1, 1994, the day NAFTA goes into effect, members of the EZLN take over seven municipal seats and hundreds of ranches in Chiapas, calling on the people of Mexico to rise up with them to overthrow the PRI.

• Though a ceasefire is signed 12 days later, the Zapatistas have continued their struggle for true democracy and autonomy in their own communities and their example has had tremendous impact both nationally and internationally. In spite of massive military presence and the increased paramilitary violence characteristic of low intensity warfare, the Zapatistas have developed alternative systems of government, education and health in their territories in Chiapas.

• After the election of President Fox, the Zapatistas march to Mexico City to demand that the new government ratify the San Andres Accords, signed with the EZLN in 1996 to recognize indigenous land and cultural rights, but never implemented by the government. Despite the mobilization of millions, the Mexican Congress passes a watered down version of the Accords, betraying any remaining hope of institutional reform.

ATENCO

- In December of 2001, the FPDT (People's Front in Defense of the Land) forms in San Salvador Atenco, a campesino community on the outskirts of the sprawling megalopolis of Mexico City. The FPDT forms in response to government plans to displace residents from their lands with minimal compensation in order to build an international airport. Resistance to these plans ends in violent confrontations that carry into 2002 as the residents of Atenco, machetes in hand, emerge victorious against an army of riot police, leading to the August 2002 cancellation of the airport plans.

- On May 3rd, 2006, members of the FPDT are attacked for attempting to sell flowers in nearby Texcoco. After a response in support of their members, federal police arrive and arrest the leadership of FPDT and hundreds of others, and sexually assault 23 women. Solidarity actions take place all over Mexico and in dozens of countries.

- After sentencing three movement leaders to 67-year prison terms, the right-wing government of Felipe Calderón announces, in 2007, the re-initiation of airport plans in Atenco.

Photography

Glossary

Atole - Traditional corn-based drink

Brigadas móviles - Mobile brigades; in the Oaxacan social movement, these brigades were often the groups responsible for seizing government buildings

Caciques - Local political bosses, usually with ties to political parties

Calenda - Parade that opens the Guelaguetza

Campesinos - Peasant farmers

Comandancia - Leaders of an organization or movement

Compas, Compañeros/as - Comrades, friends, fellow organizers

Conasupo (Compañía Nacional de Subsistencias Populares) - A welfare program distributing cheap corn

Desaparición de Poderes - Dissolution of power; legal term that refers to the mandated resignation of a municipal or state authority

Entregadores - Paramilitaries

Esquiroles - People paid by the government to commit crimes

Fiesta - Party

Gringo/a - Person from the U.S.

Guaraches - Simple leather sandals

Güero/a - White person

Guelaguetza - Literally refers to reciprocity or "the gift of giving"; it is also the name of an annual cultural, folkloric celebration which takes place in July every year in Oaxaca

Huevos - Eggs; also refers to testicles

Huipiles - Traditional indigenous blouses

Indios - "Indians," indigenous people, often a derogatory term

Ingobernabilidad - The inability to govern

La Barricada - The barricade

Magonismo - Ideology based on ideas of Mexican Anarchists Enrique and Ricardo Flores Magon

Mera mera fiesta - The real celebration

Mezcal - Alcoholic beverage made from the maguey plant, similar to tequila

Mestizo - People of mixed European and Indigenous ancestry

Mole - Popular Mexican sauce made from a variety of spices

Ni Voz, Ni Voto - Neither voice nor vote

Oaxaqueña - Oaxacan woman

Ocote - Pine wood used for burning

Oportunidades - Mexican federal welfare and reproductive health education program

Órale pues - right on; all right, then

Palacio del Gobierno - Governor's palace

Petate - Straw mat

Pistoleros - Hired assasins

Plantón - Sit-in

Plan Puebla Panamá - Neoliberal economic plan initiated in 2001 intended to develop and integrate nine southern Mexican states and Central America and Colombia

Poder popular - Popular power, the people's power

Priistas - PRI party supporters

Procampo (Programa de Apoyos Directos al Campo) - An agricultural subsidy program

Pueblos - Towns or villages, can also refer to people

Resiste - Resist

Salud - Cheers, health

Tamales - Traditional steamed cornmeal

Tapetes - Sand murals, rugs

Tequios - Collective, unpaid work for the benefit of the community

Tlacuache - Opossum

Tlayudas - Popular Oaxacan dish made with tortillas, beans, cheese and other toppings

Topiles - Alternative public security force

Usos y Costumbres - Forms of autonomous, indigenous self-governance; literally "traditions and customs"

Vámonos - Let's go

Zócalo - Main plaza in the center of Oaxaca City

Acronyms

APPO *Asamblea Popular de los Pueblos Oaxaqueños* The Popular Assembly of the Peoples of Oaxaca

ASARO *Asamblea de Artistas Revolucionarias de Oaxaca* Revolutionary Assembly of Oaxacan Artists

COMO *Coordinadora de Mujeres Oaxaqueñas 1º de Agosto* August 1 Coordinating Body of Oaxacan Women

CROC *Confederación Revolucionaria de Obreros y Campesinos* Revolutionary Confederation of Workers and Campesinos

COCEI *Coalición Obrero Campesino Estudiantil del Istmo* Coalition of Workers, Farmers and Students of the Isthmus

CODEP *Comité de Defensa de los Derechos del Pueblo* Committee in Defense of the Rights of the People

EDUCA *Servicios para una Educación Alternativa* Services for Alternative Education

EPR *Ejercito Popular Revolucionario* Popular Revolutionary Army, leftist guerilla movement in Mexico

FPR *Frente Popular Revolucionario* Popular Revolutionary Front

PFP *Policía Federal Preventiva* Federal Preventive Police

POMO *Policía Magisterial* Teachers Union Police

PRD *Partido de la Revolución Democrática* Revolutionary Democratic Party

PRI *Partido Revolucionario Institucional* Institutional Revolutionary Party

RODH *Red Oaxaqueña de Derechos Humanos* Oaxacan Human Rights Network

UABJO *Universidad Autónoma Benito Juárez de Oaxaca* Benito Juárez Autonomous University of Oaxaca

UCIZONI *Unión de Comunidades Indígenas de la Zona Norte del Istmo* Union of Indigenous Committees in the Northern Zone of the Isthmus

UNAM *Universidad Nacional Autónoma de México* National Autonomous University of MexicoThe C.A.S.A. Collectives are centers for solidarity work in Oaxaca and Chiapas, México. C.A.S.A. facilitates the work of international activists as human rights observers, independent journalists and volunteers for grassroots organizations. For more information, see www.casacollective.org.

The C.A.S.A. Collectives are centers for solidarity work in Oaxaca and Chiapas, México. C.A.S.A. facilitates the work of international activists as human rights observers, independent journalists and volunteers for grassroots organizations. For more information, see www.casacollective.org.

PM Press was founded in 2007 as an independent publisher with offices in the US and UK, and a veteran staff boasting a wealth of experience in print and online publishing. We produce and distribute short as well as large run projects, timely texts, and out of print classics.

We seek to create radical and stimulating fiction and non-fiction books, pamphlets, t-shirts, visual and audio materials to entertain, educate and inspire you. We aim to distribute these through every available channel with every available technology—whether that means you are seeing anarchist classics at our bookfair stalls; reading our latest vegan cookbook at the café over (your third) microbrew; downloading geeky fiction e-books; or digging new music and timely videos from our website.

PM Press is always on the lookout for talented and skilled volunteers, artists, activists and writers to work with. If you have a great idea for a project or can contribute in some way, please get in touch.

PM Press . PO Box 23912 . Oakland CA 94623
www.pmpress.org